H E B E R   J.

Exemplar to the Saints

G R A N T

OTHER COVENANT BOOKS
BY MATTHEW J. HASLAM:

John Taylor: Messenger of Salvation

HEBER J.

Exemplar to the Saints

GRANT

MATTHEW J. HASLAM

Covenant Communications, Inc.

Covenant.

Cover images courtesy of the Church Archives,
The Chuch of Jesus Christ of Latter-day Saints.

Cover design copyrighted 2003 by Covenant Communications, Inc.
Published by Covenant Communications, Inc.
American Fork, Utah

Printed in Canada
First Printing: November 2003

10 09 08 07 06 05 04 03   10 9 8 7 6 5 4 3 2 1

ISBN 1-59156-379-8

For Jackson,
who tried to type his name into many a chapter.

Acknowledgements

I am grateful to Melanie Joy Barrett for her research assistance and work on chapter 4. I also greatly appreciate Roger Buehner, whose timely advice made my writing career possible.

TABLE OF CONTENTS

∽ ABBREVIATIONS ∽

The following abbreviations have been used whenever citing from the sources listed below. In citing other works in the notes, short titles are used after the first full citation. Some of the quotations in this book have been standardized to reflect modern spelling, punctuation, capitalization, and grammar.

CR   Conference Report

IE   *Improvement Era*

MS   *The Latter-day Saints' Millennial Star*

Collected Discourses   *Collected Discourses Delivered by President Wilford Woodruff, His Two Counselors, the Twelve Apostles, and Others.* 5 vols. Comp. and ed. Brian H. Stuy. Burbank, Calif.: BHS, 1987–1992.

CHC   B. H. Roberts. *A Comprehensive History of The Church of Jesus Christ of Latter-day Saints.* 6 vols. Salt Lake City: Deseret News Press, 1930.

HC   B. H. Roberts, ed. *History of The Church of Jesus Christ of Latter-day Saints.* 7 vols. Salt Lake City: The Church of Jesus Christ of Latter-day Saints, 1932–1951.

JD   *Journal of Discourses.* 26 vols. London: Latter-day Saints' Book Depot, 1854–1886.

~ TIMELINE ~

22 November 1856	Heber Jeddy Grant born in Salt Lake City to Jedediah Morgan Grant and Rachel Ridgeway Ivins Grant
1 December 1856	Death of father, Jedediah M. Grant
10 June 1875	Becomes second counselor in presidency of ward YMMIA
1 November 1877	Marries Lucy Stringham in St. George Temple
30 October 1880	Called to preside over Tooele Stake
31 October 1880	Ordained a high priest by John Taylor
6 April 1880	Chosen as secretary in YMMIA general superintendency
16 October 1882	Ordained an Apostle, age 25, by George Q. Cannon
26 May 1884	Marries Hulda Augusta Winters
27 May 1884	Marries Emily Harris Wells
3 January 1893	Death of wife Lucy Stringham Grant
10 March 1895	Death of son Daniel Grant, age 3
27 February 1896	Death of son Heber Grant, age 7
Aug. 1901–Sept. 1903	Presides over Japanese mission
Jan. 1904–Dec. 1906	Presides over European mission
25 May 1908	Death of wife Emily Harris Wells Grant
27 January 1909	Death of mother, Rachel Ridgeway Ivins Grant
23 November 1916	Becomes President of the Quorum of the Twelve Apostles
23 November 1918	Becomes President of The Church of Jesus Christ of Latter-day Saints, age 62
27 November 1919	Dedicates Hawaii Temple
26 August 1923	Dedicates Alberta Temple
23 October 1927	Dedicates Arizona Temple
14 May 1945	Heber J. Grant dies in Salt Lake City, age 88
1 June 1952	Death of wife Augusta Winters Grant

⌐INTRODUCTION⌐

In describing Heber J. Grant, B. H. Roberts wrote that he "is not a highly imaginative person; intellectually speculative, or a constructive theorist, or largely a doctrinaire."[1] This assessment, Roberts pointed out, was not meant to be disparaging. Rather, it described how Heber differed from many of his fellow Church leaders and their predecessors. In addition, Roberts's observation was merely a reiteration of what Heber often admitted publicly. Speaking at the October 1895 general conference, Elder Grant commented on how much he had enjoyed the talks and then told the gathered Saints, "I take as deep if not a deeper interest in the practical every-day affairs of life and the everyday duties that devolve upon us as the ordinary man. I am naturally not very spiritually inclined, but I do take an interest in the ordinary affairs of life."[2] In this regard, Roberts suggested, Heber favored the reasoned approach of someone like St. James rather than the "rhapsodic visions [of] an Isaiah."[3]

Heber's self-appraisal was characteristic of his temperament, personality, and the way he lived his life. For Heber, religion did not consist of speculative theology but of a need for diligence; it was not idle philosophy but a day-to-day effort. He aptly summed up this approach when, in April 1922, as President of the Church, he admitted:

> I may not have been a very good preacher of the gospel of
> the Lord, Jesus Christ, from the standpoint of doctrinal
> preaching, but I have endeavored, to the best of my ability,
> since I was called as a boy forty odd years ago, to preside

over the Tooele stake of Zion, and forty years this coming
October, to be one of the Apostles of the Lord, Jesus
Christ, to preach the doctrine of St. James, "I will show
thee my faith by my works."[4]

For Heber true eloquence was not simply a matter of discourse well
spoken but a matter of a life well lived.

This philosophy clearly influenced his style as a preacher. His
speeches were generally not theological treatises but discussions of religion in the "ordinary affairs of life" that often drew upon personal
stories. At times Heber apologized for including stories "made up principally of my own experiences," but he believed this approach could
best motivate his listeners and readers to action. As he explained, "It is
admitted that statements of personal experiences, spoken or written,
carry more force, and make a more lasting impression upon the minds
of hearers and readers than can be made in any other way. This must
be my excuse for relating so many incidents in my own career."[5]

It is through the stories he told that both Church members who
lived during his presidency and those who have followed have come
to know Heber J. Grant. For so many, Heber J. Grant has become
synonymous with the famous stories of his hard-won achievements in
baseball, penmanship, and singing. These three stories demonstrate
Heber's cycle of accomplishment: 1) he desired to achieve something;
2) he faced great obstacles to begin with, often in the form of disparagement by others; 3) this disparagement then served as additional
motivation to accomplish what he desired; and 4) with a dedication
that bordered on fanaticism, he worked toward the goal. So often
Church manuals have used the three stories to illustrate what Orson
F. Whitney once said about Heber: "He is a model of perseverance, a
persistent overcomer of obstacles, a dynamo of energy, and a gatling
gun in execution."[6] And while the stories certainly do teach lessons of
persistence and perseverance, they are of interest for what they reveal
about Heber's personality, his beliefs, and how he saw his role as a
Church leader. To better understand Heber J. Grant, it is expedient to
consider both why he told these stories and how he told them.

In so many ways, Heber's speeches were demonstrations. He told
stories that showed how religious beliefs were to be lived, and in so

doing he provided models for Church members to follow. He also, at times, quite literally demonstrated what he was teaching in the process of giving the speech. This approach was nowhere more apparent than when Heber addressed a conference of the Young Men's Mutual Improvement Association (YMMIA) on 2 June 1901, when he not only discussed his efforts at learning to sing but also sang several hymns. The following excerpts from his talk show how Heber J. Grant both spoke and lived as an exemplar to the Saints.

Singing to the Saints

> I am glad to have the opportunity of addressing this conference, and I desire that my remarks may be beneficial to the young people particularly. Some of you are aware that I have been trying for a little over a year to sing to the Latter-day Saints. I have made one or two attempts in this Tabernacle, but have not always been successful. I purpose tonight to preface my remarks by trying to sing you a song. I may not succeed, because in attempting to sing, I imagine my position to be similar to that of some of our singers, should they attempt to preach.[7]

When Heber gave the speech he was nearly forty-five years old, and he was trying to learn to sing despite the fact that previous attempts had been notable failures. As a young boy, his mother tried to teach him but gave up as she found Heber couldn't carry a tune. At age ten he signed up for a singing class but had no more success than before. As Heber recalled, Professor Charles J. Thomas "tried and tried in vain to teach me . . . to run the scale or carry a simple tune, and finally gave up in despair." Thomas soon pronounced Heber's case hopeless as he came to the opinion that Heber "could never, in this world, learn to sing." Not cowered by his failure, Heber continued to practice singing, though he would do so when far away "from anyone who might hear me." His practice, however, was not followed by any measure of perfection. In fact, it was near impossible for him to sing on key. Most of the time he had difficulty getting through a single line correctly, let alone a complete verse of a favorite hymn.[8]

In his early forties Heber sought to take up singing yet again. After hearing Brother Horace S. Ensign sing, Heber suggested that he would "gladly give two or three months of my spare time if by so doing it would result in my being able to sing one or two hymns." Probably unaware of past pronouncements on Heber's singing ability, Ensign suggested that "any person could learn to sing who had a reasonably good voice, and who possessed perseverance, and was willing to do plenty of practicing." Heber replied that he had "an abundance of voice, and considerable perseverance," and he immediately sought out a lesson. The two worked on the hymn "O My Father," and they practiced singing together until Heber could sing without mistakes. "At the end of two weeks," Heber reported, "I could sing it alone, with the exception of being a little flat on some of the high notes."[9] Buoyed by his success, Heber, in the following months, incorporated his singing into his preaching. On a trip to Arizona and Mexico he sang at least one hymn in each meeting where he addressed the Saints.

Heber J. Grant as Object Lesson

> I do not want this congregation of young people to go away with the idea that I make any pretension to being a singer. I simply sing these songs as an object lesson, to show that a person who is musically deaf, and cannot distinguish the keys upon the piano, can learn to sing. Please join in the chorus, and I will sing, or try to. I have been able to sing it through in the country wards, but somehow I seem to lose my nerve here. Please join in the chorus of "Who's on the Lord's Side, Who?" Let me say before beginning that whenever I sing, as a rule, I encore myself; so, I may sing another song when I finish this one.[10]

At this point Elder Grant stopped his sermon and serenaded the audience, first with the hymn "Who's on the Lord's Side, Who?" For his encore, he sang "The Holy City."

Though he explicitly stated that his objective in singing was to prove that all can sing, it was certainly not the only purpose for the demonstration. As when he told of his accomplishments in baseball and handwriting, Heber J. Grant saw his efforts to sing as an object lesson with multiple applications. The stories clearly illustrated his persistence despite great odds, but above all, Heber wanted the Saints to see themselves as he saw himself, as one able to "act for [himself] and not to be acted upon" (2 Ne. 2:26). As he often told them, "I am thoroughly convinced that we can do nearly anything within the bounds of reason that we want to do. I believe that genius is, as has been stated by someone, 'an infinite capacity for taking pains.'"[11]

In advocating these beliefs, Heber was not merely offering the Saints self-help advice or demonstrating that anyone could get ahead if he or she but worked hard enough. Rather, Heber believed there was a decidedly religious component to his admonishment to work and succeed. "We are the architects of our own lives," Heber taught, "not only of the lives here, but the lives to come in the eternity." If the Saints failed, he believed, they alone were responsible as they had "all the ability, all the knowledge, all the power that is necessary, faithfully, diligently, and properly to discharge every duty and every obligation that rests upon them."[12] The recognition that "we are the architects . . . [and] the builders of our own lives"[13] was not only a determinant in worldly success but one of eternal significance. So while Heber certainly saw value in learning the hymns of Zion, there was an even more important lesson to be taught.

Acknowledging Failure as Well as Success

I had an object in view in singing to you tonight; it was that I want to impress our young boys particularly to learn to sing. I believe that we can accomplish any object that we make up our minds to, and no boy or girl ought to sit down and say, because they cannot do as well as somebody else, that they will not do anything. God has given to some people ten talents; to others, he has given one; but they who improve the one talent will live to see the day when they will far outshine those who have ten talents but fail to improve them. Musically speaking, I doubt if I possess one talent. Maybe I have half of one; that is about all. Let me tell you the difficulties I have labored under, so that you may know what I have had to overcome. I was requested some months ago, at President Cannon's, to sing "God Moves in a Mysterious Way," and simultaneously, I was requested to sing, "O My Father." I heard the first request, but not the second. I turned to President Snow's wife and said, "Will you kindly play that tune for me in the key of F." (Prof. C. J. Thomas very kindly took a book and wrote the keys in which I ought to sing, because I cannot sing in the key in which songs are written, my voice being too low.) Sister Snow very kindly consented to play for me. She heard the request for "O My Father," so she played the prelude to that. When she finished playing the first verse, I began singing "God Moves in a Mysterious Way." As good fortune would have it, the first three notes of these two songs are the same, when "O My Father" is sung in the old tune. . . . When I began to sing "God Moves in a Mysterious Way," the audience laughed, though I did not know why they were laughing at a hymn of this kind. Sister Snow, realizing what I was about, changed the music to "God Moves in a Mysterious Way," and we got through with the hymn all right.[14]

When he used personal examples to teach the Saints, Heber did not do so merely for self-aggrandizement, or as he explained it, "for the purpose of throwing bouquets at myself."[15] Admittedly his stories about baseball and penmanship were success stories—his team won the territory championship, and he became professor of penmanship at the university. Indeed, he saw nothing wrong with success, once confessing, "There is something in being at the head that has always favorably impressed me."[16] More important, however, he sought to emphasize that success came after great difficulty and at the risk of failure and embarrassment.

Heber took a certain pleasure in recounting the struggles he had faced, and in so doing he was more than willing to laugh at himself and his foibles. At the April 1901 general conference, he apologized for "having persecuted people as I used to" with singing.[17] In another speech he recalled practicing singing at Brother Ensign's workplace, which was located next to a dentist's office. When a group of young people passed by the office and heard the singing, they "remarked that it sounded like somebody was having his teeth pulled."[18]

Heber also willingly acknowledged how his attempts to sing became the object of good-natured ribbing by his colleagues in Church leadership. One Church official, upon hearing him soon after Heber began singing lessons, commented that Heber's singing was much like Orson Pratt's poetry: "He said Brother Pratt wrote only one piece of poetry, and this looked like it had been sawed out of boards, and sawed off straight."[19] On another occasion, Heber went to meet with a fellow member of the Twelve who greeted him by saying, "Come in, Heber, but don't sing." When this same elder later taught patriarchs that the only way to gain the spirit of their office was by giving blessings, Heber asked how he was to learn to sing if not by singing. The elder conceded that Heber was correct, but added: "Sing every chance you get, Brother Grant, but do your first singing down in Mexico or Arizona or somewhere a long way off."[20] Even in their council meetings Heber was the butt of their jokes. "In our meetings in the Temple the brethren would say 'That is as impossible as it is for Brother Grant to carry a tune,' and that settled it; everybody acknowledged that was one of the impossibilities."[21]

On a trip to Arizona Heber was able to exact some small measure of revenge on two of his fellow brethren in the Twelve. During their travels Heber asked Elders Rudger Clawson and J. Golden Kimball if they objected to his singing a hundred hymns during the day. Supposing that the request was made in jest, the two elders consented. Heber recalled their response: "We were on the way from Holbrook to St. Johns, a distance of about sixty miles. After I had sung about forty times, they assured me that if I sang the remaining sixty they would be sure to have nervous prostration." Heber, however, was not one to give in quite so readily. "I paid no attention whatever to their appeal, but held them to their bargain and sang the full one hundred."[22] The criticism and ridicule were not enough to dissuade Heber from his goal. In fact, the "uncomplimentary remarks" from his "nearest and most intimate friends" only furthered his resolve. As he said, "It only increases my determination to learn to sing."[23]

In his speeches he emphasized his persistence despite repeated failures. In returning home from a trip to Arizona and Mexico he desired to "give an object lesson to the young people, and to encourage them to learn to sing." Although he had success singing while touring the southern stakes and branches, Heber's performance at the YMMIA conference was less than exemplary. "I made a failure," he admitted, "getting off the key in nearly every verse, and instead of my effort encouraging the young people, I fear that it tended to discourage them."[24] This conference was not the first time Heber's attempts resulted in failure. At the April 1901 general conference, he had made a similar effort. Following this attempt he announced, "I regret that I failed in my object lesson. I would have been glad had I been able to sing that song through without a mistake. I have only sung it through five times today without a mistake, but when I tried it the sixth time I got an error in it. But I haven't got over my nervousness when standing before the assembled people to sing." Notwithstanding his nervousness, Heber worked hard and continued to sing in Church meetings. For him "to try and fail" was "a perfect annoyance."[25]

The Necessity of Work

When I was learning to sing, "I Have Read of a Beautiful City," I practiced that song one day twelve times at one sitting. There are three verses in it; so I sang thirty-six verses, and by actual count I made five mistakes to a verse, which made 180 mistakes in one practice, and I knew nothing about it. When I first began to learn to sing, it took me from three to four months to learn two simple hymns. I learned a hymn a few weeks ago in three hours—half an hour's practice every evening for six days, and I had it all right.

I mention this to show you the force of what some man has said, that which we persist in doing becomes easier for us to do—not that the nature of the thing is changed, but that our power to do is increased. I desire the boys to learn that their power to do will increase if they only go to work.

[You] do not have to say in the mission field, "We are very sorry, but we can't sing, and we wish we had a companion that could." You can all sing, if you are not tongue-tied, and I have proved it.[26]

For Heber accomplishing a goal meant one thing: work, lots of hard work. At the April 1901 conference he explained his goal to someday sing in the Tabernacle without making a mistake. Though he believed, as did Alma, that God "granteth unto men according to their desire" (Alma 29:4), he did not suppose God would merely grant his wish. As he told the Saints, "I desire to sing, and I expect to work at it and to stay right with it until I learn."[27] And work he did. He sang his first hymn hundreds of times before he finally got it right. He explained, "One hundred and fifteen songs in one day and four hundred in four days, is the largest amount of practicing I ever did."[28] At one point, his singing practice monopolized his time. He told the *Improvement Era* audience, "When I first commenced to write for the *Era,* it was my intention to become a frequent contributor, but during the past few months, I have neglected writing for the reason that my spare time has been devoted to practicing singing."[29] For Heber work was a virtue, and nothing great could be accomplished without it, a characteristic he hoped to make plain in recounting examples of his own efforts.

Exemplar to the Saints

Perhaps I have said enough on singing for one night. I had an ambition to sing "The Holy City" before I left for Japan, and to do it in the big Tabernacle, and my ambition has been gratified. Whether I sang it well or not, I am not prepared to say, because my musical ear did not tell me; but I have sung it, and I leave the result as an object lesson. God has said that the song of the righteous is a prayer unto him, and it shall be answered with a blessing upon their heads. He also says that he rejoices in the song of the righteous. I say to you, praise God in the songs of Zion, and he will bless you, because he has promised to do so.[30]

As an example to the Saints, Heber J. Grant had no interest in simply being perceived as the leader others thought he should be. On several occasions he told of a letter he received from his boyhood friend Richard W. Young, who pleaded for him not to sing. "I admit that your point is a good one, *i.e.,* if *you* can learn to sing, *nothing* need discourage *anybody*—but the fact that success ultimately must be reached by traveling along the border-land of ridicule, makes the task a difficult and delicate one, particularly for an Apostle, who, unlike the ordinary musical crank, cannot afford to cultivate his thorax at the expense of his reputation as a man of judgment."[31] Young's point might have been a good one had it been addressed to someone other than the recipient. But Elder Grant wasn't concerned with his public reputation if it meant appearing to be something he was not. Horace G. Whitney, who had once been in Heber's employ, suggested that if "Heber J. Grant [were] ground up, after the manner of ore at one of our valley sampling mills" and a sample submitted for analysis to "the most expert microscopist or analyst," it would be impossible "to discover the slightest trace of hypocrisy."[32]

In this regard, Heber had little concern for any sense of false dignity. One day a friend noticed him carrying home a bucket of milk from the tithing office and suggested that he wasn't "maintaining [his] dignity as an Apostle, the president of a bank and of other institutions by walking through the streets carrying a bucket of milk." Heber disagreed with the statement and replied, "There are some people that spend all their time trying to maintain their dignity, and there are other people that can push a wheelbarrow or carry a bucket of milk through the streets, and nobody dare step on their dignity. I hope I am one of the latter kind."[33] For Heber a reputation as a man of judgment was not to be obtained by hiding or by being other than he was, but by revealing to all that the private Heber was the same as his public persona.

The honesty and genuineness in the way Heber J. Grant spoke and lived was readily apparent throughout his tenure as prophet. In his April 1928 conference address, President Grant admonished "the Saints to try to shape their affairs so that they can occasionally go to the temple."[34] While such counsel was expected of a prophet, what may have been unexpected was the following admission: "For years I felt that I was too busy to find a day or an evening in which to go to the temple." However, he had come to the realization that "inasmuch as I could find time to play golf nearly an hour or two that I could find time to go to the temple for at least once a week."[35] Beginning in 1927, Heber had set the goal to attend the temple weekly, which he had been able to do "by planning my affairs, by staying away from lectures or concerts or theatres or operas."[36] In January of the following year he had decided to double his weekly attendance, and by April he had attended the temple nearly thirty times.

For Heber J. Grant "there [was] nothing like [an] example,"[37] and an example is what he sought to be. He never saw himself, however, as a paradigm of perfection, an ideal to be imitated in all things. If anything, he was a paradigm of effort. And though he didn't consider himself to be "spiritually inclined" by nature, he worked hard to become a remarkable example to the people he led.

NOTES TO INTRODUCTION

1. *CHC*, 6:485.
2. *Collected Discourses*, 5:59.
3. *CHC*, 6:485.
4. CR, April 1922, 5.
5. Heber J. Grant, "The Nobility of Labor," *IE*, December 1899, 82.
6. Noble Warrum, ed., *Utah since Statehood: Historical and Biographical*, vol. 2 (Chicago and Salt Lake City: S. J. Clarke Publishing, 1919), 15.
7. Grant, "Farewell Address of Apostle Heber J. Grant," *IE*, July 1901, 683.
8. Grant, "Learning to Sing," *IE*, October 1900, 886.
9. Ibid., 887.
10. Grant, "Farewell Address of Apostle Heber J. Grant," 684.
11. Grant, "On Going to the Temple," *IE*, August 1941, 459.
12. *Collected Discourses*, 4:357.
13. CR, April 1939, 16.
14. Grant, "Farewell Address of Apostle Heber J. Grant," 684–85.
15. Grant, "The Nobility of Labor," 82.
16. CR, April 1908, 56.
17. CR, April 1901, 63.

18. Grant, "Learning to Sing," 887.
19. Ibid.
20. CR, April 1901, 63.
21. Ibid.
22. Grant, "Learning to Sing,"889.
23. Ibid., 887.
24. Ibid., 888.
25. CR, April 1901, 62–63.
26. Grant, "Farewell Address of Apostle Heber J. Grant," 685–86.
27. CR, April 1901, 63.
28. Grant, "Learning to Sing," 889.
29. Ibid., 886.
30. Grant, "Farewell Address of Apostle Heber J. Grant," 687–89.
31. Grant, "Learning to Sing," 887–88; emphasis in original.
32. Warrum, *Utah since Statehood: Historical and Biographical,* 14.
33. "Heber J. Grant," *IE,* February 1930, 284.
34. CR, April 1928, 8.
35. Grant, "A Family Temple Night," *IE,* July 1944, 425. Though he clearly wanted to be a model for the Saints, Heber did not try to whitewash his failings. In addition to stating the good he accomplished, he was ever one to reveal his shortcomings. In a letter to his nephew, which was published in the *Improvement Era,* he acknowledged, "I have sadly neglected my temple work." He recognized that "as I am seventy-one years and past, unless we do something in the near future, I am going to pass on to the other side and meet my relatives who have died without a knowledge of the gospel and am going to be condemned for my neglect."
36. CR, April 1928, 8.
37. Grant, "On Going to the Temple," 459.

~ ONE ~

It was evening, and a young boy, only six years old, was returning from school. He walked down Main Street in Salt Lake City. On one side of the street were the buildings belonging to Brigham Young. On the opposite side sat a home that had once been teeming with family members yet now stood empty. The prominent lot, located on what had been designated Wilford Woodruff's block, had been given to the boy's father back in 1847, and by February of the following year two log houses had been erected.[1] The buildings had been home to his father, a widower, who shared them with his oldest half sister, as well as six wives who joined the family in the next eight years.

As the boy sat down on the step leading into the yard, tears welled up in his eyes and soon he was openly crying. Circumstance had not seemed to favor the boy. Born on 22 November 1856, Heber Jeddy Grant never knew his father, who, at the age of forty, died just nine days after his son's birth. Although Heber's father, Jedediah M. Grant, had enjoyed positions of prominence within the community—he had been mayor of Salt Lake City and Brigham Young's Second Counselor in the First Presidency—his status had not led to financial security for the boy and his mother. Following a brief marriage to her former husband's brother, which had proved disastrous because of the man's burgeoning alcoholism and which was dissolved by Brigham Young after two years,[2] the boy's mother and several other sister wives remained in the Main Street home until finances dictated otherwise. The small estate was eventually divided up, and his mother, with Brigham Young's approval, purchased a small adobe home at 14 Second East Street.[3]

Distraught over the loss of what once was, Heber continued to cry. Then, with a determination that would characterize his childhood and adolescence, he stood up and glared at the old house. Shaking his fist at his former home, Heber cried out, "When I am a man I will buy you back." Though eventually he would fulfill this promise made in desperation, for the time being Heber and his mother lived lives of privation.[4]

A Determined Mother

Rachel Ridgeway Ivins Grant, an adept seamstress, attempted to support her son by sewing. The work, however, did not always provide for their basic needs. So destitute were they at times that during the winter they would retire to bed early because they could not afford to have a fire, relying on "bed-clothes to keep us warm."[5] Food was not always plentiful, and Heber recalled "when four pounds of sugar was the family's supply for the entire year." For them, butter "was an almost unknown luxury." One Christmas, Rachel cried because she could not afford to buy her son even a stick of candy for a present.[6]

Despite their obvious want, financial assistance was always refused by the fiercely independent Rachel. While visiting her sister Anna in St. George, Rachel encountered Brigham Young. Knowing the financial straits of his former counselor's last wife, he offered Church assistance. Rachel, however, was adamant in her reply: "I . . . told [Brigham Young] that persons had said to me I was a fool for working as I did when [Jedediah] killed himself working in the kingdom. I told him I did not wish to be supported by the Church. I was too independent for that."[7] Accepting assistance was simply not an option. On another occasion, her bishop offered to use fast offering money to repair her leaky roof. Rachel replied, "Oh, no, you won't. No relief money will ever put a roof on my house. I have sewing here. When I get through

Jedediah Morgan Grant, Heber J. Grant's father.

with this sewing that I am now doing, I will buy some shingles and patch the holes, and this house will take care of me until my son gets to be a man and builds a new one for me."[8]

Though Rachel had "a fine sewing hand," the work was painstakingly slow and "she found it impossible to get ahead." Together Rachel and Heber decided to save all they could in order to purchase a new sewing machine. "Denying themselves all but the bare necessities of life," mother and son eventually scrimped enough to buy the machine.[9] The purchase would bring them even closer together. After sewing all day at someone else's home, Rachel would return to the small house and prepare the evening meal. After supper, she had Heber clear the table to make room for the sewing machine and would then return to work. To aid her, Heber "sat on the floor at night until midnight and pumped the sewing machine to relieve her tired limbs."[10]

Rachel's independence and striking determination was magnified by what she had given up when she joined the Church. Religious by nature, Rachel, like many other early converts to the Church, had sought a religion that addressed her spiritual needs. She described herself as "religiously inclined but not of the long-faced variety. I thought religion ought to make people happier and that was the kind of religion I was looking for." She experimented with the Quakers, but found them lacking in the substance she wanted and was saddened that they did not allow hymn singing. "The spirit often moved me to burst out in songs of praise, and it was with difficulty that I could refrain from doing so."[11] At the age of sixteen she joined the Baptists with the consent of her guardians (her parents had passed away when she was young). The Baptists had more of what she was looking for, but she did not enjoy their loud sermons.

Latter-day Saint missionaries began preaching in her area in New Jersey, and at first Rachel had no desire to listen to them. However, her older sister, Anna, joined the Church, and finally Rachel was persuaded to attend some meetings and listen to the missionaries. But she initially did not find their teachings appealing. Heber related, "The night after attending her first Mormon meeting on a Sunday she got down on her knees and prayed the Lord to forgive her for doing such a wicked thing as going to listen to false prophets on the Sabbath." Curiosity prevailed long enough for Rachel to continue attending these meetings, until finally she was challenged by her Baptist minister. "Miss Ivins," he said, "you went to hear those awful Mormons. If you go to hear them again your pew in my church will be vacant." The statement had the reverse effect than the minister intended. "What the minister said to my mother got her 'Dutch' up, and she said to him, 'My pew is vacant in your church. I shall go to hear these Mormons, and I shall pray. It may be that they have the truth.'"[12]

Rachel proceeded with her investigations of Mormonism. "I commenced to read the *Voice of Warning* and the Book of Mormon. I read nearly all night in the Book of Mormon, and felt that it was true."[13] As she explained, "A new light seemed to break in upon me, the scriptures were plainer in my mind, and the light of the everlasting Gospel began to illuminate my soul." In addition to reading the scriptures, another experience confirmed her growing faith. She related:

> While thus investigating, a little child died whose mother had joined the Latter-day Saints. The Baptist minister preached about it, regretting that its parents had neglected to have it baptized and thereby it was lost and could not have salvation. Afterwards Elder [Orson] Hyde preached the funeral sermon and portrayed the glories of our Father's kingdom and the saved condition of the little innocent ones who died before they came to the years of accountability—"For of such is the kingdom of heaven." The contrast was very great. I was steadily being drawn into the Gospel net.

The threat of disfellowship by the Baptist church offered another stark contrast with the Mormons and provided the final decisive factor. "One wanted to hold me against my convictions, and the other was free salvation without money and without price. I soon handed my name [to the Mormons] for baptism and rendered willing obedience to the first four requirements of the Gospel of Jesus Christ as revealed through the Prophet Joseph. . . . And, oh, what joy filled my being!"[14]

At the time of her baptism, her brothers tried to dissuade her from converting by offering "to settle an annuity upon her that would make her independent, so that she could have everything she needed every day of her life, if she would renounce her faith." Otherwise, the uncles never wanted to see her again. Emphasizing just how they saw the religion, they told her, "If you had become a common street-walker, a strumpet, we would not feel any worse about it than we do about your joining those awful 'Mormons.'"[15] With her departure, the brothers did extend an invitation to return at any time if she would but renounce her faith. And with such a renunciation, the previous financial offer was to be restored. Although in need of the money as a young mother, Rachel was never willing to meet the stipulated condition.

Mother and Son

Rachel's independence, determination, and work ethic were clearly passed on to Heber as he was given all "the advantages of poverty."[16] As a fourteen-year-old still attending school, Heber learned about insurance and decided that he needed to insure his mother's home. For the following twenty weeks, Heber worked each Saturday to raise the necessary money to cover the premium. When Heber's bishop in the Salt Lake Thirteenth Ward, Edwin D. Woolley, heard of his effort, he remarked, "My gracious, Heber ought to have given that ten dollars to his mother. Why, if Widow Grant's house were to burn

down I would go around this ward, and she has so many friends that within forty-eight hours I would get the money with which to build her a better house than the one she now has." Knowing, however, that there were many who would come to their aid was not good enough for Heber, and when he heard of the bishop's comment he replied, "I

Heber J. Grant, age nine, and his mother, Rachel.

can insure my mother's house for enough to build another one if it burns down and I don't care to live in a house built by charity. I would be a little pauper, living in a house not knowing who furnished the money to build it, and therefore not being able to pay it back."[17]

Despite all the assistance Heber gave his mother, Bishop Woolley labeled Heber the "laziest boy in the Thirteenth Ward." In part, this designation arose from Heber's work to fulfill a promise that he had made to himself. Growing up the only child of Rachel—his siblings came from Jedediah's other wives—Heber "learned to sweep, and to wash and wipe dishes, but did little stone throwing, and little indulging in those sports which are interesting and attractive to boys, and which develop their physical frames." He grew, as he described himself, "long and lanky," but he did not fill out. When he joined a local baseball club he was physically underdeveloped, and his skills were nonexistent. He could neither run nor hit well, and he could not throw the ball from one base to another. This inability to throw often prompted taunts from the other boys as they would shout, "Throw it here, sissy!" when he fielded the ball. His abilities, or rather inabilities, relegated Heber to play with the youngest boys on the "third nine" when the boys his age and older played on the "first nine." While Heber's efforts provided a good deal of comic relief for the other ballplayers, he did not succumb to their derision or his physical limitations. Rather, he related, "I solemnly vowed that I would play baseball in the nine that would win the championship of the Territory of Utah."[18]

Saving money from shining the shoes of his mother's boarders, Heber purchased a baseball and went to work. He told his mother of his personal pact to play on the championship nine, and she provided the needed encouragement to see the promise come to fruition. Heber spent hours and hours throwing the new ball against his neighbor's barn. It was when the neighbor, Bishop Woolley, saw Heber's persistence "in coming home from school and throwing a ball at [the] barn" that Woolley declared him to be the "laziest boy" in the ward. The support from Heber's mother, however, was undeterred, and he recalled, "She would tie up my arm at night with wet clothes because it would ache so badly."[19] The pain was such that it made it difficult at times for him to sleep at night. Eventually he developed such accuracy that he could hit "most any adobe [brick] on

[Woolley's] barn that I wanted to." He also "hired a boy to throw at me until I could catch so well that I challenged the second nine to stand in a row with me and have the swiftest thrower throw at us, and as a fellow missed a ball he had to sit down. I stood up until all the second nine had missed. I then said that I did not propose to play in a club that they considered the third nine when I could make the second nine all sit down."[20]

Heber continued to practice and eventually earned a spot on the "first nine." And just as he had promised himself, his Red Stocking team won the territorial championship. With his goal accomplished, Heber promptly retired from playing, or as he explained years later in parlance of the financial world, he quit "while my credit was still good."[21] It was not a love of the sport that drove Heber, but a love to achieve. Looking back on his playing days, he readily acknowledged all "the hours and days, and weeks and months partially wasted by me, with the sole object of learning to be a baseball player."[22] Yet he was grateful for "having a mother that realized it was wise to encourage her boy athletically or otherwise, to help him to do something that he had an ambition to do,"[23] and he recognized the one thing he "accomplished by my experience as ball player, namely, the fulfilling of a promise made to myself."[24] It would not be the last time that Heber would be spurred on by failure to set and achieve a goal that was seemingly out of his reach.

A close relationship with his mother, grounded in complete love and devotion and forged in the furnace of economic hardship, led Heber to feel bound to her "with cords of steel." As he would explain, "I doubt if a mother and son were ever any nearer, for she was both father and mother to me."[25] This relationship became a guiding force in his life, one that he would put above even his own desires.

Growing into adolescence, Heber held out hopes of obtaining a university education, an opportunity that was increasingly available to young men in America. One day Heber met George Q. Cannon, who was the territorial delegate to Congress. Cannon inquired if Heber would like to go to the Naval Academy or West Point. When he indicated a preference to go to Annapolis and join the navy, Cannon told him that he would get him "the appointment without competitive examination." The opportunity so excited him that he was unable to sleep much that evening. Rather, he said, "I lay awake nearly all night long rejoicing that the ambition of my life was to be fulfilled." Finally he fell asleep just before dawn, and he had to be woken up by his mother. He immediately related to her the good tidings. "Mother, what a marvelous thing it is that I am to have an education, as fine as that of any young man in all Utah." But then Heber noticed that his mother had been crying, she having already heard the news. About this experience Heber subsequently commented: "I have heard of people who when drowning had their entire life pass before them in almost a few seconds. I saw myself an admiral in my mind's eye; I saw myself traveling all over the world in a ship, away from my widowed mother." Clearly recognizing the implications of such a commission, he laughed and embraced his dear mother. "Mother," he exclaimed, "I would not go to Annapolis for all the education and all the glory of all the world. I am going to be a businessman and shall enter an office right away and take care of you, and have you quit keeping boarders for a living."[26] Staying in Salt Lake, Heber gave up his formal educational aspirations, and he soon traded the classroom for a business office.

A Budding Businessman

The statement "I am going to be a businessman" was somewhat inaccurate in terms of the verb tense he used. Heber's entrepreneurial efforts had begun at a young age. For some years he had been shining shoes to bring in needed money. He had also set out with his good friend Heber Wells to raise chickens. Intending to sell the eggs, the boys' efforts were stymied when the chickens refused to lay. What Wells would later call "a keen inborn business sense" even pervaded Heber's recreational pursuits. In contrast to his initial ineptness at baseball, Heber was quite skilled at marbles. Playing a game known as "Knuckle Down Boston," he was rivaled by only one other boy in the neighborhood, and their matches always "drew a large gallery of spectators." When playing for "keeps" with the other neighborhood boys, Heber would return home with "pockets frequently bulged with his winnings." The marbles then became the currency with which Heber paid these same boys to do chores around his house. When Bishop Woolley saw the other boys working at Widow Grant's, he assumed that Rachel "had to hire her chores done because her own coddled son was not disposed to do them." Here was yet another reason for the bishop to consider Heber lazy.[27]

It was while playing a game of marbles that Heber came to the conclusion that his shoe-shining business had limited possibilities. Heber and a friend were engaged in a match when the latter pointed out a bookkeeper at Wells Fargo and commented that he made $150 a month. Quickly figuring out the man made six dollars a day, Heber was notably impressed. Earning a nickel for each pair of shoes he shined, he realized he would have to shine an awful lot of shoes to earn such a lofty sum. Resolving to become a bookkeeper, Heber pledged to himself that he would one day likewise work for Wells Fargo.[28]

With Heber, goals were not merely wishes or something he might get around to one day. Rather, they required immediate action. He enrolled himself in a bookkeeping class taught at the Deseret University, located just a few blocks from his Salt Lake home. Just as his teammates initially laughed at his baseball skills, Heber "remember[ed] the amusements I furnished my fellow-students." His penmanship was atrocious. "One remarked when looking at my books, 'What is it, hen tracks?' Another said, 'Has lightning struck an ink bottle?'" Heber acknowledged that these statements were made in jest, as part of "good natured fun." Yet notwithstanding the students' intentions, the statements "cut deep." Much like his baseball days, the hurt Heber felt did not lead him to abandon his aspirations but instead became a source of motivation. Instead of seeking to play on the champion nine in baseball, Heber now resolved "to live to set copies for all who attended the university, and to be the teacher of penmanship and bookkeeping in that institution."[29] Thus, he dedicated his spare time to practicing his handwriting. This practice did not take place just on occasion but was pursued systematically and relentlessly. There were many times when he "plied his pen until after midnight, only to rise again before six in the morning to continue his writing before regular business hours."[30]

Midway between his fifteenth and sixteenth birthdays, he quit school to work as a bookkeeper and policy clerk at H. R. Mann and Company Insurance Agents—his writing had improved to the point where he was now qualified for the position. Yet Heber was still not satisfied with his abilities, and he continued to "'scribble' when not otherwise occupied." Heber not only quickly learned his responsibilities but also was so proficient in carrying them out that he often had nothing to do. As he worked in the same building as A. W. White and Company's Bank, he soon began volunteering "to assist with the bank work, and to do anything and everything that I could to employ my time, never thinking whether I was to be paid or not, but only having a desire to work and learn." His eagerness impressed those with whom he worked, and the bank's bookkeeper, Mr. Morf, took him under his tutelage. Morf "took the pains to assist me in my efforts to become a proficient penman."[31]

While still in his teens, Heber become such a fine penman that he was soon supplementing his regular salary with the money he made writing greeting cards, wedding invitations, insurance policies, stock certificates, and legal documents. One New Year's Day a man paid him twenty dollars, better than a quarter of his monthly wages, to write "Happy New Year" and the man's name on nearly five hundred greetings cards. So proficient had he become with his pen that while still working for H. R. Mann and Company he received an offer to triple his salary if he would move to San Francisco and work as a penman.[32]

One year at the Utah Territorial Fair he passed by an exhibit that displayed the work of professional penmen. With the confidence that came from accomplishment, he boasted to the man running the art exhibits that as a sixteen-year-old he could write better than any of the men whose work was displayed. The man laughed and suggested that "nobody but a cheeky insurance agent would make such a remark." Guilty as charged, Heber nonetheless backed up his boast. He paid the three-dollar entrance fee, procured a writing sample, and then told the man that "if your judges know good penmanship when they see it I will get the diploma." The judges concurred with Heber, and "he walked away with the diploma for the best penmanship in the Territory."[33]

Heber continued to be a proficient employee and found that he could readily complete his responsibilities before the day was through. While he was working as a bookkeeper and policy clerk for Henry

Wadsworth, an agent of Wells Fargo, he volunteered to perform extra assignments. He continued to gain experience in the banking industry as he assisted the bookkeepers and tellers at Wells Fargo. He also assisted Wadsworth by keeping the books for the Sandy Smelting Company, which Wadsworth had been doing on his own. So pleased was Wadsworth with his young employee that he hired him to do collecting for Wells Fargo, paying him twenty dollars a month in addition to his regular monthly salary of seventy-five dollars. Even more important for Heber was the fact that he accomplished his goal to one day work for Wells Fargo.

However, Heber never quite felt comfortable in his employment with Wadsworth. As he would later tell his boss, he volunteered for assignments "because I had nothing else to do, and I did not like to sit around idle." Even with the additional work, Heber did not feel that he was earning what he was being paid. Rather than continue on in this position, he resolved one New Year's Eve that he would approach his boss the following Monday morning and tell him, "I have decided to give you thirty days' notice and quit this job. I feel that I am not earning the money that I am being paid."[34] He was at the office that evening writing out greeting cards to sell the next day when Wadsworth returned and inquired what he was doing. He told his boss, "I am getting ready for the harvest tomorrow. Last year I made $20.00 on New Year's Day by writing calling cards. Had I had 'Happy New Year' already written on them I am sure I would have made $25.00; so I am going to be prepared for the harvest tomorrow."[35] His employer commented that "it never rains but what it pours," and gave him a hundred-dollar New Year's bonus, telling Heber, "Nobody else in the office will get a dollar, because all the other employees watch the clock to see how quickly they can get out, but you come back here nights, frequently, and you have done a lot of work for me personally, which you volunteered to do."[36] Whereas the "average employee likes to get out of the office," he continued, you "seem to like to work."[37]

With the bonus in hand, Heber decided that he wouldn't resign the following week. Though pleased with the money, he was even more grateful his employer had acknowledged his dedication and resourcefulness: "The satisfaction enjoyed by me in feeling that I had

Heber J. Grant and his brothers. Front row (left to right): Jedediah Morgan, Joseph Hyrum, and George Smith Grant. Back row (left to right): Brigham F., Heber J., and Joshua F. Grant.

won the good will and confidence of my employer was worth more to me than twice one hundred dollars."[38] The next day, Heber set up a small table in James Dyer's Book Store and sold his cards. Working from ten in the morning to three that afternoon netted Heber $37.50. As he would later comment, "It was the same pen (Spencerian No. 1), the same ink, the same hand, and the same eye that guided the pen, when, in the university, according to my fellow students, I made ink look as if lightning had struck an ink bottle."[39]

When Wadsworth was transferred to work for Wells Fargo in San Francisco, Heber purchased the insurance company for five hundred dollars, money he obtained when his mother mortgaged her home. The assets which he purchased "consisted entirely of goodwill, or the inside track in securing policy renewals."[40] With no guarantees, Heber had to convince insurance companies to issue policies through him and persuade customers they ought to continue with a salesman not yet of age. To solidify his situation, Heber formed a partnership with another Salt Lake insurance agent, B. W. E. Jennens.[41]

While waiting for profits to come in from his insurance company, Heber sought out other employment. As had been his goal as a young bookkeeping student, Heber became professor of penmanship and bookkeeping at the University of Deseret, located at the corner of First North and Second West Streets in Salt Lake. One student,

George D. Pyper, recalled Heber "going from seat to seat inspecting the work of the pupils." Heber's "Spencerian style," Pyper remembered, "became my model and many reams of paper were used up with his copy before me."[42]

During the middle of 1877, Heber, not yet twenty-one, was appointed assistant cashier at Zion's Savings Bank and Trust Company. The bank's president, Brigham Young, had cajoled the other board members to hire the boy when the previous assistant cashier was called away on a Church mission. It was only because Heber had "volunteered to help the cashier, the tellers, and the book-keepers" at A. W. White and Company and at Wells Fargo and had learned the banking "business from A to Z" that he was qualified for the position at Zion's.[43] As he was required to give a $25,000 bond vouching for his honesty, Heber sought the signature of the man who had hired him. Confidently he went to the president at his office, arriving there just as Brigham was heading out the door. Heber explained, "President Young, as you know, the other day I was elected assistant cashier of Zion's Savings Bank and Trust Company, and they require a bond of $25,000, guaranteeing my honesty. I thought it would be a very appropriate thing for the president of the bank to sign my bond and I have come up for your signature." Not taken aback by Heber's boldness, President Young smiled and replied, "Heber, I don't see how in the world I can get out of signing your bond. I said so many good things about you at the directors' meeting, if I now refuse to sign your bond they will accuse me of not telling the truth." Agreeing to sign the bond later, as he was then leaving for a carriage ride after a long day of business, Brigham Young never put his signature to the document. Rather, he returned home from the ride ill and died within days.[44]

Not only was Heber assistant cashier at the bank, but he was also the "the janitor, the bookkeeper, the paying and receiving teller, and the collector of interest on notes after bank hours." Each business day he opened the bank at ten in the morning and closed at three in the afternoon, for which he received a monthly salary of seventy-five dollars. As he was earning two to three times that amount from his insurance business, he indicated that he would never have worked for the paltry sum "had it not been that it gave me a chance to talk insurance to the depositors."[45] A consummate salesman at heart, he took it upon himself to talk up insurance whenever he could, even insuring three clients while they all watched firemen extinguish a large Salt Lake fire.[46]

Shortly after the previous assistant cashier returned from his mission, Heber was surprised one day to read in the *Deseret News* of his own resignation from the bank. As Brigham Young was no longer the bank's president, the board members sought to reinstate Heber's predecessor. Though shocked by the change in his standing, Heber responded in what was now becoming typical fashion: he turned adversity into further motivation and drive. Concerning his termination at Zion's, Heber later suggested, "I am half inclined to think that the kicking me out of the Savings Bank was the making of me as it started me out to rustle with greater energy than ever before."[47]

Already driven to succeed, the oft-failing but ever-achieving Heber now had further need to demonstrate his worth. As a salesman he was teeming with energy. One morning at his office, Heber and his partner discussed whether or not twenty-five dollars could be made if the whole day was devoted to soliciting new policies. After assuring his partner that he could double that amount, Heber left the office at nine in the morning. When he returned at seven that evening he had sold almost $31,000 worth of insurance. The profits for his firm amounted to just over $101. His workday was not yet complete as he stayed at the office until after ten at night.[48] With such efforts and success, Heber's salary at Zion's would seem even more trivial in comparison with what he was soon to earn.

NOTES TO CHAPTER 1

1. Gene A. Sessions, *Mormon Thunder: A Documentary History of Jedediah Morgan Grant* (Urbana: University of Illinois Press, 1982), 73.

2. Ronald W. Walker, "Rachel R. Grant: The Continuing Legacy of the Feminine Ideal," in *Supporting Saints: Life Stories of Nineteenth-Century Mormons,* ed. Donald Q. Cannon and David J. Whittaker (Provo, Utah: BYU Religious Studies Center, 1985), 29. Rachel married George Grant on 17 February 1858. According to Walker, "President Young

promised the Grant wives that if they would remain as a unit and accept George Grant, Jeddy's brother, as their new husband, they would successfully raise their children to be faithful Mormons. Rachel and several of the Grant wives complied."

3. Ibid.

4. Heber J. Grant (hereafter cited as Grant), "My Days in School," *IE,* November 1941, 665. Regarding his pledge Heber explained, "I often thought of that years later when I formed a syndicate and bought $350,000 worth of ZCMI stock, and part of the ZCMI store was built on the ground where that first home stood."

5. Grant, "Faith-Promoting Experiences," *MS,* 19 November 1931, 760.

6. "Two Octogenarians," *IE,* November 1936, 667.

7. Rachel Ridgeway Grant to Heber J. Grant, 19 October 1901, Family Correspondence, Grant Papers, Historical Department Archives, The Church of Jesus Christ of Latter-day Saints, Salt Lake City; quoted in Walker, "Rachel R. Grant," 40 n. 37.

8. Grant, "Address," *Relief Society Magazine,* October 1937, 626; Grant, "One Man's Memory of an Honored Mother," *IE,* May 1936, 268.

9. Mary Grant Judd, "A Mormon Wife: The Life Story of Augusta Winters Grant," *IE,* February 1946, 88.

10. Grant, "Faith-Promoting Experiences," 760.

11. Leonard J. Arrington and Susan Arrington Madsen, *Mothers of the Prophets* (Salt Lake City: Deseret Book, 1987), 114.

12. Grant, "One Man's Memory of an Honored Mother," 267.

13. "Statement of Rachel Ridgeway Grant," *IE,* November 1930, 48.

14. Arrington and Madsen, *Mothers of the Prophets,* 112.

15. Grant, "Faith-Promoting Experiences," 759.

16. Judd, "A Mormon Wife," 121.

17. Grant, "One Man's Memory of an Honored Mother," 268.

18. Grant, "Work, and Keep Your Promises," *IE,* January 1900, 196.

19. Grant, "One Man's Memory of an Honored Mother," 268.

20. "Heber J. Grant," *IE,* February 1930, 284.

21. Ibid.

22. Grant, "Work, and Keep Your Promises," 197.

23. "Heber J. Grant," 284.

24. Grant, "Work, and Keep Your Promises," 197.

25. Judd, "A Mormon Wife," 88.

26. Grant, "For the Love of My Mother," *IE,* May 1942, 271.
27. Heber M. Wells, "President Grant—The Business Man," *IE,* November 1936, 687.
28. Grant, "The Nobility of Labor," *IE,* December 1899, 82.
29. Ibid., 83.
30. Richard L. Evans, "President Grant—As 'Jim the Penman,'" *IE,* November 1936, 702.
31. Grant, "The Nobility of Labor," 83.
32. Evans, "President Grant—As 'Jim the Penman,'" 702.
33. Ibid.
34. Grant, "For Service Rendered," *IE,* March 1940, 137.
35. "Heber J. Grant," 284.
36. Grant, "For Service Rendered," 137.
37. "Heber J. Grant," 284.
38. Grant, "The Nobility of Labor," 86.
39. "Heber J. Grant," 284.
40. Ronald W. Walker, "Young Heber J. Grant: Entrepreneur Extraordinary," in *The Twentieth Century American West: Contributions to an Understanding,* ed. Thomas Alexander and John F. Bluth (Provo, Utah: Charles Redd Center for Western Studies, 1983), 93.
41. Ibid., 94.
42. Evans, "President Grant—As 'Jim the Penman,'" 702.
43. Grant, "Dream, O Youth! Dream Nobly and Manfully," *IE,* September 1941, 524.
44. Wells, "President Grant—The Business Man," 687.
45. Grant, "Dream, O Youth! Dream Nobly and Manfully," 524.
46. Walker, "Young Heber J. Grant: Entrepreneur Extraordinary," 95.
47. Heber J. Grant to George T. Oddel, 30 January 1892, Letterpress Copybook, 12: 735–36, Grant Papers, Historical Department Archives, The Church of Jesus Christ of Latter-day Saints, Salt Lake City; quoted in Walker, "Young Heber J. Grant: Entrepreneur Extraordinary," 97.
48. Rachel Grant Taylor, "Portrait of a Young Man," *IE,* November 1938, 703.

TWO

Near the end of his life, President Heber J. Grant would recall that as a precocious seventeen-year-old, "I dreamed in my mind about my future life—what I was going to do until I became thirty-five." For Heber, dreams were more than mere whims; they required planning and work. With aspirations in both politics and business, he decided that by his mid-thirties he would hold political office and be president of a corporation. Heber set intermediate goals to accomplish along the way. Most relevant for the teenager were three goals he wanted to achieve before he turned twenty-one: to be in business for himself, to build his mother a new house, and to get married. Reflecting back on this time, President Grant could proudly observe, "I had planned everything I was going to do and where I was going to get, and from the time I was seventeen until I was twenty-four years old I accomplished every one of the things that I had planned to do and dreamed about in my mind and worked for."[1]

In the realm of finances, his goal to be in business for himself was accomplished with over a year to spare when he purchased the H. R. Mann Insurance Company. Not only was he working for himself, he was, before his twenty-second birthday, immensely successful. Whereas an average salary in Utah was between $400 and $600 a year, Heber earned $3,800 the first year after he turned twenty-one. In 1879 he followed that up by making $5,480 and more than $6,800 in 1880.[2]

Given the sacrifices his mother had made and the poor circumstances in which they had found themselves, Heber longed to provide his mother with a better place to live. When she had refused Bishop Woolley's assistance to fix the leaky roof, Rachel confidently asserted

that her boy would someday build her a new home. With his low esti-
mation of Heber's work ethic, Bishop Woolley was confident Rachel
would never have a decent house. Heber would later report that the
bishop's statement provided the impetus for this goal. And when it
was finished, before he was twenty-one, Heber invited his bishop to
the home to offer the prayer of dedication.[3]

By marrying Lucy Stringham on 1 November 1877, Heber
completed his third goal with just three weeks to spare. Initially Lucy
wanted to wait until spring to travel to St. George for the wedding.
But as an insurance salesman, Heber did "not know what 'No'
means." And with the perseverance that his job demanded, "he kept
at it, and finally she surrendered."[4]

At age twenty-three, Heber was well on his way to accomplishing
the other objectives he had set out to achieve by his thirty-fifth
birthday. There was one thing that he hadn't planned for: Church
service. "I had never thought of holding a Church position; I had
other plans."[5] Growing up he repeatedly told his mother, "I do not
want any Church position. I want to be a business man."[6] Heber's
reticence should not be construed as proof of deviation from the
Church. He simply had not set out to follow in his father's footsteps
as a prominent Church leader. Although he had set his sights on
success in the business world, Heber's early years provided him with a
remarkable religious education, one that would enable him to succeed
in later Church callings.

Mentors in Church Leadership

From his earliest days, Heber had the privilege of knowing
personally many of the Church leaders. While he yet lived in his
father's home on Main Street, his neighbor on the north was Daniel
H. Wells, the man who replaced his father as Brigham Young's counselor in the First Presidency. To the immediate south lived Edward
Hunter, who served as Presiding Bishop from 1851 until his death in
1883. According to Heber's description, they were "two of as God-
fearing, kind, splendid men as ever drew the breath of life." And he
felt very fortunate for the chance to grow up "under their tutorship to
a certain extent."[7]

Heber was also a welcomed visitor in Brigham Young's home. As a six-year-old, Heber decided one winter day that he would hop aboard the back of President Young's sleigh. His plan to ride only for a block or so and then jump off and walk home was foiled as the sleigh quickly picked up steam. "President Young was driving such a fine team . . . that I dared not let go, hence rode on till we reached the

Heber J. Grant as a young boy, ca. 1860.

Cottonwood, and then when the sleigh slowed up, to pass through that stream, I jumped off." It was only then the prophet spied the nearly frozen youngster and had him brought into the wagon and placed under a buffalo robe. "After I got warm he inquired my name, and told me about my father, and his love for him. He told me to tell my mother that he wanted her to send me up to his office in six months to have a visit with him; and in six months I went for the visit."[8] From that time on Heber remained an intimate of the Young family.

The trips he made to the prophet's residence at the Lion House were numerous. Heber was even welcome at the Young family prayer. When he would hear the bell ring signaling prayer time, he would be off. "Quite frequently I would run through our back lot across through Brother George A. Smith's lot and across the street, and kneel down in President Brigham Young's home at family prayers."[9] Whereas many knew Brigham Young as a prophet and statesman, Heber became acquainted with him as a private man and father. These visits enabled him to witness the prophet supplicate the Lord on family and personal matters. "On two occasions," Heber recalled, "when [Brigham] was praying I turned and looked. It seemed as though he had the Lord right there talking to him and asking him what he wanted and telling him what he needed."¹⁰ Young Heber would also visit the Lion House when running errands or when he had to deliver a message to the Young household. Often Eliza R. Snow, or "Aunt Eliza," would invite him in for a brief visit. It was during these brief conversations, Heber recalled, that "she told me scores and scores of faith-promoting incidents in her life in Nauvoo when she was there as a girl with my mother, and incidents in the life of the Prophet Joseph Smith."¹¹ The closeness to the Young family provided Heber with a religious education that few in the Salt Lake Valley enjoyed.

The Impact of the Thirteenth Ward Meetings

The 1860s and 1870s were a time of organization and reorganization in the Church. As the Relief Society had been previously disbanded, Eliza R. Snow was called in 1867 to be president of the women's organization. Brigham Young directed her to oversee the reestablishment of the Relief Society in each of the Salt Lake wards. It wasn't until 18 April 1868 that Bishop Woolley called Rachel Grant to be the Thirteenth Ward Relief Society president, a calling she held for thirty years. As a result, Heber "grew up as a little boy in the Relief Society meetings," which brought him into regular contact with Emmeline B. Wells, Eliza R. Snow, Zina D. Young, and "other leading women of the Relief Society."¹² It was from these women, many who had known the Prophet Joseph personally in Nauvoo, that Heber heard over and over the testimonies they had of the Restoration. (See appendix 1.)

The year before the Relief Society was reorganized in the Thirteenth Ward, Brigham Young, George Q. Cannon, George A. Smith, and Daniel Wells met with ward leaders to formalize the Sunday School program. While various wards had previously conducted Sunday schools, the 30 March 1867 meeting with Bishop Woolley was designed to establish a program that all wards might subsequently follow. Initially, the schools taught academic subjects, but Church leaders subsequently altered the curriculum so it focused on moral, religious instruction.¹³ A regular attendee, Heber excelled at these academic exercises, particularly in memorizing the Articles of

Faith, the Word of Wisdom, or part of John Jaques's *Catechism*.[14] A fellow student reminded Heber, "You were our prize Sunday School boy. Bros. Musser and Mabin predicted great things for you."[15] Not only was Heber an exemplary student, the teacher and class had a significant effect on Heber's life. Said Heber, "I know that many times I have poured out the gratitude of my heart to Hamilton G. Park, who was the teacher of my Sunday School class in my boyhood and young manhood days. I shall never get over thanking this man for the wonderful impression for good that he made upon me and for the remarkable testimonies he bore in our classes, telling his experiences as a missionary, and the blessings and power of God that attended him while proclaiming the Gospel on two missions to . . . Scotland."[16]

Developing a "Practical" Testimony

Entering into adolescence, Heber had never read the entire Book of Mormon. He believed it was true, but this understanding was based on the witness of his mother and other teachers like Hamilton Park. Rachel Grant had repeatedly encouraged her son to read through the book systematically but had failed in her efforts to motivate him. However, when Heber was about fourteen, his uncle issued a challenge to his son, Anthony C. Ivins, and Heber. The first to read the Book of Mormon was promised a pair of ten-dollar buckskin gloves—a substantial prize. As Heber recalled, "Any boy of fourteen who had a pair of those gloves thought he was 'it.'"[17] With insight beyond his years, Heber recognized that to win the gloves would require him to read so quickly he would benefit little from his reading. He decided to concede the gloves to his cousin and carefully read twenty-five pages a day. The day after the boys began reading, Heber had read his determined amount while his cousin was already 125

Heber J. Grant as a young man.

pages ahead. "I went on reading twenty-five pages a day and occasionally I got so interested that I read fifty or seventy-five pages, and lo and behold, I got through first and got the gloves."[18] It was during the first night of reading that Heber read the story of Nephi and his remarkable faith. As Heber later explained, "I read the Book of Mormon as a young man, and fell in love with Nephi more than with any other character in profane or sacred history that I have ever read of, except the Savior of the world. No other individual has made such a strong impression upon me as did Nephi." Heber greatly admired Nephi's determination to accomplish—despite the apparent obstacles—that which the Lord commanded (see 1 Ne. 3:7). For this reason Nephi was one of the "guiding stars" of his life.[19]

As a young man Heber regularly attended meetings in the old bowery.[20] When the Tabernacle was completed, he typically found an aisle seat about two-thirds of the way back for each of the semiannual general conferences.[21] He was even a regular attendee at meetings in the Salt Lake Thirteenth Ward at a time when only 10 to 15 percent of ward members participated in the main Sunday meeting.[22] It was during one of these ward meetings that Heber had one of his most profound spiritual experiences as a boy. After Heber listened to "a very gifted sermon by a finely educated man who had a marvelous command of language,"[23] Brother Millen Atwood rose to speak, and Heber quickly noted the "grammatical errors in his talk." An assignment for the grammar class he attended two evenings a week required that he bring in four sentences that were not grammatically correct, along with the corrections. With Atwood's speech Heber was sure to get "enough material to last me for the entire winter in night school grammar class." He wrote down the first sentence and "contemplated making my corrections and listening to . . . Atwood's sermon at the same time." After the first sentence, however, Heber wrote no more—"not a word." With the sermon complete, Heber found "tears of gratitude and thanksgiving . . . welled up into my eyes because of the marvelous testimony which that man bore of the divine mission of Joseph Smith, the Prophet of God." Later, President Grant stated that Atwood's "testimony made the first profound impression that was ever made upon my heart and soul of the divine mission of the Prophet. I had heard many testimonies that had pleased me and made their impression, but this was the first testimony that had melted me to tears under the inspiration of the Spirit of God to that man."[24]

The result of these experiences was that Heber developed a practical faith in the gospel. As one close friend observed, "He lives his religion but is seldom able to warm himself unto enthusiasm over a principle; his love is practical, everyday, common-sense devotion to principles which from their superiority to all others, he chooses to believe are divine."[25] This practical faith was aptly illustrated by an experience he had at a Thursday fast meeting (the regular day for such meetings at the time). During the service Bishop Woolley sought donations from ward members, and afterward Heber approached him and gave him fifty dollars. The bishop took five dollars out and returned the remainder, indicating that Heber need not pay any more. Heber then responded, "Bishop Woolley, by what right do you rob me of putting the Lord in my debt? Didn't you preach here today that the Lord rewards fourfold? My mother is a widow and she needs two hundred dollars." The bishop, probably somewhat taken aback by the response, replied, "My boy, do you believe that if I take this other forty-five dollars you will get your two hundred dollars quicker?" When Heber acknowledged that he did, Woolley kept the balance of the fifty dollars. Heber later recalled:

> While walking from that Fast meeting to the place where I worked, an idea popped into my head. I sent a telegram to a man asking him how many bonds of a certain kind he would buy at a specified price within forty-eight hours and allow me to draw a draft on him through Wells-Fargo's bank. He was a man whom I did not know and I had never spoken to him in my life, but I had seen him a time or two on the streets of Salt Lake. He wired back that he wanted as many as I could get. My profit on that transaction was $218.50.[26]

On Sunday Heber was pleased to report to the bishop that he had been rewarded fourfold, though he did have to come up with $3.35 in order to pay a full tithe.

As Heber's testimony developed, not all of his religious experiences were uplifting. As a seventeen-year-old, he was called in to see the President of the Church in his office.[27] President Young indicated that it was now time for Heber to consider a mission. The boy concurred but suggested that his older half brothers ought to be called first. When Heber's siblings refused, Young again asked to see Heber. The youngest Grant boy subsequently agreed to accept a call at the following conference. Both Heber and Rachel recognized that a mission call would fulfill a promise made in his patriarchal blessing that Heber would enter the ministry while yet young. He prepared for the call by reading accounts of other teenage missionaries, and with great anticipation he attended April conference in 1876. The call, however, never came. Only years later did Heber learn that members of the Twelve whom he knew intimately, Daniel H. Wells and Erastus Snow, objected to the call, suggesting the boy was already serving an admirable mission in supporting his mother. Failing to receive a mission call, however, caused Heber to doubt his patriarchal blessing and the purported inspiration that had directed it. "I was tempted seriously," he wrote, "for several years to renounce my faith in the Gospel because this blessing was not fulfilled. The spirit came over me . . . that the patriarch had lied to me, and that I should throw the whole business away."[28]

It was Heber's participation in the Sunday School program and the Young Men's Mutual Improvement Association that made the difference at a time when, he explained, "I stood as it were upon the brink of usefulness or upon the brink of making a failure of my life." The lessons taught, the associations with Church leaders and friends, and the testimonies heard in these programs played a significant role in helping Heber become "a faithful member of the Church of Christ."[29] And while these experiences, which included some leadership responsibilities, helped build his testimony, it is difficult to imagine he would have felt prepared for what lay ahead.

A New Stake President in Tooele

October 1880 began somewhat inauspiciously for Heber J. Grant. On Thursday the fifth he journeyed by horseback to Park City. On his return trip he noticed some beautiful fall leaves, which he desired to take home to his wife of nearly three years. He gathered the leaves and climbed aboard his horse. The trip home, though, divested him of his collection, with the last of the leaves falling into some mud as he got off his mount. Losing the leaves, however, proved providential for Lucy as the beautiful leaves turned out to be poison ivy. On the seventh, Heber recorded in his journal that "poison ivy broke out." So severe was his reaction to the plant that it restricted his actions such that he "did little or no work" in the ensuing days. The illness subsequently confined him to bed from the eighteenth to the twenty-eighth of the month. Even when his second daughter, Lucy, was born on the twenty-second, Heber hardly had the strength to make his way to his wife's bedroom to see the infant.[30]

By the thirtieth, Heber was well enough to make an unexpected trip to Tooele, thirty-six miles west of Salt Lake City. Concerning his trip, Heber unceremoniously noted in his journal: "1 October, visited Tooele City in company with President John Taylor, George Q. Cannon, and Joseph F. Smith, and Elders George F. Gibbs and W. W. Taylor." The purpose for the visit was to attend the Tooele stake quarterly conference led by Francis M. Marion. In one meeting, the twenty-three-year-old Grant addressed the assembly for only a "few minutes." He was followed by the Second Counselor in the First Presidency, Joseph F. Smith, "whose discourse," Heber observed, "was very interesting." Probably even more interesting for both Heber and the Tooele Saints was President John Taylor's following address. He arose and announced that the First Presidency and the Quorum of the Twelve had called Heber J. Grant to be the new stake president. When the congregation was asked to sustain him, Heber was quick to notice that while "there were no negative votes" for him, "a goodly number of the saints did not vote for the new president."[31] Heber later suggested that John Taylor, both of his counselors, and Elder Francis Lyman (his predecessor as stake president) all attended the conference because "they thought it needed an immense amount of authority to put in a young man as the president of that stake."[32]

President Taylor then asked Heber to speak to his new charges. The new stake president approached the pulpit and proceeded to speak for all of seven and a half minutes. He told the people of Tooele "everything I could think of, and some of it over twice," and then he

ran out of ideas and sat down. With some in the audience ques-
tioning why an inexperienced outsider was being brought in to lead
the stake, the speech did little to win over their confidence. President
Grant admitted to them that he "knew nothing of the duties that
devolved upon me, but with the help of the Lord I would do the best
I could, and that with His help I had no fear at all but what I could
get along." When someone later suggested that he had ruined his
credibility by admitting such, Heber countered by saying, "Well, they
may discover that I have a little sense, later on, and that will agreeably
surprise them."[33]

Though an accomplished salesman, Heber, as he reported again
and again during his tenure as a General Authority, was not much of
a public preacher. Faithful as a block teacher (what now would be
called a home teacher) with Hamilton Park, never missing a monthly
visit,[34] he, however, had done almost none of the actual teaching. And
while he had been serving as a Sunday School teacher of adolescents
at the time of his call, he had no confidence in his ability to address
the members of his new stake. As he later said, "[I] was a boy, without
experience, never having spoken in public in my life, for any length of
time, never ten minutes at once." In spite of his trepidations, he did
promise the people that

> there should not be a man in Tooele County who had no
> more means than I had who would do more for building
> meetinghouses, who would do more for any public enter-
> prise in that county, than I would do; that there should not
> be a man in that county who would live the Word of
> Wisdom more strictly than I would; that there should not be
> a man there who would be a more conscientious tithepayer;
> and that I would do everything the equal of any other man,
> as far as my ability would allow me to do, that I required of
> any other man.

Summing up this philosophy, he would later say, "I am a firm believer
in saying 'Come on' instead of saying 'Go.'"[35]

When the meeting concluded, Heber joined Presidents John
Taylor and Joseph F. Smith for lunch. As they sat at the table,

President Smith commented on Grant's speech: "Heber, you said you believe the Gospel with all your heart, and propose to live it, but you did not bear your testimony that you know it is true. Don't you know absolutely that this Gospel is true?" President Smith was caught off guard when Heber directly admitted that he did not: "What, you! a president of a stake?" Heber expressed his own incredulity at the notion, "That is what I said." President Smith turned to President Taylor and announced his recommendation: "I am in favor of undoing this afternoon what we did this morning. I do not think any man should preside over a stake who has not a perfect and abiding knowledge of the divinity of the work in which we are engaged." Clearly feeling overwhelmed by his calling, Heber voiced his assent: "I am not going to complain." He did not, however, get his wish. Rather than agreeing with his counselor, President Taylor began to laugh. "Joseph, Joseph, Joseph, he knows it just as well as you do. The only thing that he does not know is that he does know it. It will be but a short time until he does know it."[36] This understanding did come, and it was acquired on the job—clearly one reason why later in life Heber heartily approved of Brigham Young's belief that "more testimonies c[o]me to people while upon their feet than on their knees."[37]

President Smith was not the only person to question Heber's call. That Saturday night, after the meetings had concluded, President Grant overheard one stake member make known his displeasure with the prophet's choice: "It is a pity if the General Authorities have to send a man out here to preside, if they could not find one in Tooele County, that they could not have sent one with sense enough to talk at least ten minutes, and that they had to send a boy to preside over us." Heber later reported thinking that he was the only one with the right to complain about his call.[38] However, not all stake members shared this man's feelings. Another brother approached President Grant after one meeting and told him, "Every particle of strength and all of the ability that I as an individual possess I pledge to you. I realize what a great task it must be for you as a young man to be called upon to preside over an entire stake of Zion, and you can count on me for the very best that is in me."[39] The following day Heber was particularly gratified when Elder Lyman presented the Church authorities for sustaining. As he wrote in his journal, "I did not notice that there was any falling off in the votes when my name was presented as there had been the day before."[40]

Rather than immediately call his counselors, it was suggested that President Grant wait until he could get to know the members of his stake.[41] To that end he immediately began visiting the wards and branches. Each week he was called upon to address the congregations. But he found no more success than he had in speaking during the conference: "I ran out of ideas in five, six, and six and a half minutes."[42] Clearly recognizing his shortcomings as a preacher, the following week he chose several "excellent preachers" to accompany him to the small town of Vernon, where the ward met in a small log meetinghouse. As the men rode south from Tooele to the meeting place, Heber commented several times to Bishop John C. Sharp that it appeared that "there is nobody going to meeting." When the men reached a ridge and could see the meetinghouse, it was surrounded by wagons, yet there was no one in sight. While Heber may have wished that no one would be there to hear his short oration, as the men entered a couple of minutes before 2:00 P.M. they found the entire congregation already seated.

When it was President Grant's turn to speak, he got up expecting "to make my little speech of five, six or seven minutes." Much to his great surprise, his talk went on for forty-five minutes, and he spoke "with as much freedom and as much of the Spirit of the Lord as I have ever enjoyed in preaching the gospel." He was thrilled by the experience—he was finally able to provide the spiritual guidance that members needed, and he was rewarded personally through the witness of the Spirit. That evening "I could not restrain the tears of gratitude which I shed that night, as I knelt down and thanked God for the rich outpouring of His Holy Spirit, for the testimony that had come into my heart and soul, confirming the knowledge that I had of the gospel, giving me increased power, because of the knowledge that I had that God, by His Holy Spirit, had inspired me to proclaim this gospel."[43]

Believing that his speaking troubles were behind him, Heber traveled the following week to Grantsville, home to the largest ward in the stake. He told the Lord that he would like to speak as he had done the week previous in Vernon. Thinking that was all he had to do, he got up before the Grantsville Saints expecting to give a substantial discourse. As with the previous week, President Grant was surprised by the result: this time, however, he spoke for only five minutes. Whereas in Vernon he had experienced the liberty of speaking by the Spirit, in Grantsville, he explained, "I sweat as freely, I believe, as if I had been dipped in a creek, and I ran out of ideas completely. I made as complete a 'fizzle,' so to speak, of my talk, as a mortal could make." In place of gratitude, he felt humiliated and ashamed. Leaving the meetinghouse, Heber walked several miles out into the fields where no one could see him. As with the previous week, he sought out the Lord, but this time it was to seek forgiveness for "my egotism." "I asked God to forgive me for not remembering that men cannot preach the gospel of the Lord Jesus Christ with power, with force, and with inspiration only as they are blessed with power which comes from God."[44]

While President Grant was making these initial ward visits, he received a telling letter from his close friend Richard W. Young—a grandson of Brigham Young—who at the time was attending West Point. Having just been informed of Heber's new call, he sought to congratulate him. He then went on to acknowledge the challenges that Heber would face.

> Financially you are perhaps not to be congratulated; but, Hebe, finances sink into the most abject insignificance compared with the great compliment that has been paid your ability and the reward with which your faithfulness and integrity have met. I cannot tell you with what feelings almost of selfishness that I had not been the one in whom it pleased the Twelve to repose so much confidence. . . .
>
> I suppose, of course, that you realize the magnitude of your office: you have been called to assume the control of a stake which all good Mormons concede to be more in need of an able, live, and efficient president than any other in the Church. Outside of Church and religious significance, the high position to which you are called is one to which many

more experienced men than you could consistently aim, but when we consider, my dear friend, that ours is the Kingdom of the Almighty Ruler of these vast Universes, that we are the handful of people out of billions on the globe to whose care the conduct of His immediate plans is given, that you have been selected by His representatives on the earth, to be the leading mind and spirit of that stake which a few years ago was thought to demand the strongest president of them all, have you not more than great cause to be thankful? Indeed you have, Hebe. I consider it the most flattering success ever attained by any young man of our people. Of course, this will be a crusher to many of your business plans, and it may not be the most pleasant thing in the world to think of moving, either, for you or "Loo."[45]

When his call was first issued, Heber offered to give up his prospering insurance business so that he could properly minister to the Saints in Tooele. Instead, the First Presidency recommended that he move his family to Tooele while continuing to maintain his business interests. For the first six months of his presidency, this arrangement meant that he would arise early on Saturday morning to catch the 7:00 A.M. train to Tooele, perform his Church service, and then return home to his family and work on Monday. Finally in April 1881, Heber paid nine hundred dollars for a home in Tooele. After spending several weeks fixing up his new home, transporting his household goods by train, and unpacking, he recorded in his journal for Saturday, 14 May 1881: "Worked until train time in house and then went to the depot and met my wife and two children."[46] Even though his family now resided in Tooele, President Grant's travels largely remained the same—he performed his Church service on the weekends and returned to Salt Lake during the week to take care of his business affairs.

President Grant's service would come at a significant financial cost. His income of over six thousand dollars decreased by two-thirds, and whereas his income fell precipitously, his expenses did not. His calling necessitated that he "keep a team and hire a boy to take care of it."[47] The stake membership exceeded three thousand and covered all of Tooele County in Utah. As some of the original settlers from Tooele had moved into southern Idaho, President Grant was also responsible for the wards and branches surrounding Oakley, Idaho. To visit these outlying areas required a trip of seven to fourteen days during which Heber traveled and preached. On his last trip to Idaho as stake president he boarded a train for Ogden on a Thursday afternoon, accompanied by Elders Francis M. Lyman and John Henry Smith of the Twelve. Following the train trip and sixty-five miles by wagon, the men arrived in Oakley on Friday just after six that evening. Saturday and Sunday meetings in Oakley were followed by meetings each of the next four days in Little Basin, Albion, Cassia Creek, and Almo Valley. Leaving the last branch late Thursday afternoon, he arrived home Friday evening, having traveled "40 miles by team, 10 miles [by] horseback and 139 by rail."[48]

In addition to these traveling expenses, the stake president now found himself expected to financially contribute to the Church where he lived and where he worked. "I had to pay donations in Tooele and in Salt Lake, because in Salt Lake they said, 'You make your living here; you ought to help us.'" The calling was such a financial strain that he told Elder Lyman, "I would be simply delighted if they would call me on a mission for ten years, with the privilege after ten years of going back to Salt Lake to be born again, financially speaking, instead of being buried alive out here. I can never get out of this job as long as I behave myself. I am stuck here forever." Even though President Grant openly admitted at the time and subsequently that "I did not want the job," resigning was not an option. As he explained, he "took it for granted that the Lord wanted me to go [to Tooele] or Brother Taylor would not have been inspired to call me there."[49]

The calling also challenged him spiritually. Much as President Taylor anticipated, Heber developed a personal witness regarding the gospel, such that in expressing his concerns to Elder Lyman, he told the Apostle, "I know the Gospel is true, and I will stick with [the calling]."[50] Yet it did not come easy. His continual unease in speaking to the Saints was suggested in his journal during this time, as he noted down dutifully how long he spoke and how well. On the last trip to Idaho, for instance, he preached for twenty-seven minutes during the Sunday meeting in Oakley, and he "felt good liberty in talking to the [branch members]." The following day in Little Basin, he stood up and spoke for eighteen minutes, and again noted, "I felt good freedom in speaking, I don't know that I ever felt better."[51] In comparison, Heber commented in his journal that Elder John Henry Smith preached for thirty-seven minutes and Elder Lyman for thirty-nine.

For all his initial reluctance and continued doubts about his ability, Heber thrived in his efforts as stake president. When he was released on 29 October of 1882 to accept a call to the Quorum of the Twelve, with his first counselor Hugh S. Gowans replacing him in Tooele, Heber was able to look back on his experience with a good deal of contentment.

> I hope when I get through my labors as an Apostle that I shall have as much pleasure in looking back over the same, as I do when recalling my labors for the past two years in Tooele. Not that I have a great deal to be thankful for or praise for my own labors, but the kindness and respect and the aid and assistance that I received from my brethren and the support of the people is something that I will always remember with feelings of pleasure as well as gratitude. There is a pleasure which a person has when looking back over missionary life and experiences that is almost beyond the person's power to explain.

> I do not think that among any other people but Saints that a young man could have had the same experience as I had in Tooele. Looking at things naturally the people should have been disgusted at having a young man called to preside over them who could only talk from five to eight minutes; instead of being disgusted they endeavored to help me out by being as faithful as possible. There were exceptions to this rule, but I am glad to say that they were few and far between. The people of Tooele County will always have a warm place in my affections; especially will this be the case with the brethren with whom I was most closely associated.[52]

NOTES TO CHAPTER 2

1. Heber J. Grant, "Dream, O Youth! Dream Nobly and Manfully," *IE,* September 1941, 524.
2. Ronald W. Walker, "Young Heber J. Grant: Entrepreneur Extraordinary," in *The Twentieth Century American West: Contributions to an Understanding,* ed. Thomas Alexander and John F. Bluth (Provo, Utah: Charles Redd Center for Western Studies, 1983), 97.
3. Grant, "One Man's Memory of an Honored Mother," *IE,* May 1936, 268.
4. Grant, "Dream, O Youth! Dream Nobly and Manfully," 524.
5. Ibid.
6. CR, April 1935, 13.
7. CR, April 1932, 10.
8. CR, April 1917, 23.
9. CR, April 1932, 10.
10. CR, October 1941, 11.
11. Grant, "To Those Who Teach Our Children," *IE,* March 1939, 135.
12. CR, October 1941, 11.
13. Ronald W. Walker, "'Going to Meeting' in Salt Lake's Thirteenth Ward, 1849–1881: A Microanalysis," in *New Views of Mormon History,* ed. Davis Bitton and Maureen Ursenbach Beecher (Salt Lake City: University of Utah Press, 1987), 151.
14. Ronald W. Walker, "Young Heber J. Grant's Years of Passage," *BYU Studies* 24 (spring 1984): 134.
15. Belle Whitney Sears to Heber J. Grant, 20 February 1919, General Correspondence, Grant Papers, Historical Department Archives, The Church of Jesus Christ of Latter-day Saints, Salt Lake City; quoted in Walker, "Young Heber J. Grant's Years of Passage," 134.
16. Grant, "To Those Who Teach Our Children," 135.
17. Grant, *Gospel Standards,* comp. G. Homer Durham (Salt Lake City: Deseret Book, 1976), 350.
18. Ibid., 350–51.
19. Grant, "Dream, O Youth! Dream Nobly and Manfully," 524.
20. CR, April 1911, 21.
21. CR, April 1917, 25.
22. Walker, "'Going to Meeting' in Salt Lake's Thirteenth Ward," 155.
23. CR, April 1901, 64.

24. Grant, "The Spirit and the Letter," *IE*, April 1939, 201.

25. Richard W. Young Diary, November 1882, 2:3–4, Western Americana, Marriott Library, University of Utah, Salt Lake City; quoted in Walker, "Young Heber J. Grant's Years of Passage," 149.

26. Grant, "The Privilege of Obedience," *IE*, August 1939, 157; see also CR, October 1941, 11–12.

27. For a detailed account of this story, along with a complete listing of citations, see Walker, "Young Heber J. Grant's Years of Passage," 142–44.

28. Quoted in Walker, "Young Heber J. Grant's Years of Passage," 144.

29. *Collected Discourses,* 4:329.

30. Rachel Grant Taylor, "Portrait of a Young Man," *IE*, November 1938, 655.

31. Ibid.

32. Grant, "Criticism," *IE*, April 1941, 203.

33. Grant, "Significant Counsel to the Young People of the Church," *IE*, August 1921, 870.

34. Walker, "Young Heber J. Grant's Years of Passage,"139.

35. Grant, "Criticism," 255.

36. Grant, "Some Things for Our Young People to Remember," *IE*, July 1939, 393.

37. Grant, "The Place of the Young Men's Mutual Improvement Associations in the Church," *IE*, July 1912, 875.

38. Grant, "Some Things for Our Young People to Remember," 393.

39. Grant, "Criticism," 203.

40. Rachel Grant Taylor, "Portrait of a Young Man," *IE*, November 1938, 655.

41. Heber's two counselors, Hugh S. Gowans and Thomas W. Lee, were called at the next quarterly conference held 29–30 January 1881.

42. Grant, "Some Things for Our Young People to Remember," 393.

43. Grant, "Significant Counsel to the Young People," 870–71.

44. Ibid., 871–72.

45. Rachel Grant Taylor, "Portrait of a Young Man," *IE*, November 1938, 700.

46. Rachel Grant Taylor, "Portrait of a Young Man, Part II, The Young Family Man," *IE*, December 1938, 717.

47. Grant, "Criticism," 203.

48. Rachel Grant Taylor, "Portrait of a Young Man, Part III," *IE*, January 1939, 60.

49. Grant, "Criticism," 203.

50. Ibid.

51. Rachel Grant Taylor, "Portrait of a Young Man, Part III," *IE,* January 1939, 13.

52. Ibid., 60.

⌐THREE ↝

On the morning of 10 October 1880, the same month Heber J. Grant was called as stake president, Elder Orson Pratt announced to the general conference audience that the time had come for the First Presidency to be finally reorganized. Just as the Quorum of the Twelve guided the Church for three years following the death of Joseph Smith, the Twelve, led by John Taylor, had assumed the same role since Brigham Young's death on 29 August 1877. While explaining that the Twelve had been justified in their actions, Pratt indicated that they all clearly recognized "the necessity of this First Quorum of all Quorums of the Church again being filled up, so that the revelations of God may be honored and we fulfil their requirements." He went on to add, "Every time we thought upon the subject we saw that one Council, the most important of all, was still vacant."[1] Acting on the need to reorganize the quorum, John Taylor was chosen as President of the Church, and he was sustained by the priesthood quorums and the congregation. George Q. Cannon, Taylor's nephew, and Joseph F. Smith, Hyrum Smith's son, were selected as counselors.

The calling of the new First Presidency left three vacancies in the Quorum of the Twelve. Pratt announced that "two persons have been selected from among the High Priesthood to partially fill that vacancy in the Council of the Apostles. The third one has not yet been chosen to completely fill the vacancy in the Apostles' Quorum; we, however, may be prepared to act on that today, and we may not."[2] The two chosen—Francis M. Lyman and John Henry Smith—were called during the conference and subsequently set apart. As it turned out, the Church leadership was not prepared to take any action concerning the third vacancy for some time.

Two years passed and not only had the remaining vacancy yet to be filled, but an additional one had also opened up upon the death of Orson Pratt. At the semiannual conference in October 1882, Heber J. Grant joined his fellow Saints at the Tabernacle. Just prior to the meeting Sunday morning, he ran into George Teasdale, a man over twice his age. Brother Teasdale reached out to shake his hand and commented, "Brother Grant, I am delighted to see you." He went on to announce, "You and I are going to be"—but stopped there. His face reddened, and he failed to complete his thought. Any perplexity caused by Teasdale's action was short-lived, as the Lord revealed to Heber what Teasdale had planned to say: they were both going to be "sustained this afternoon as Apostles of the Lord Jesus Christ to fill the vacancies in the Quorum." The answer, according to Heber, "went through me like a shock of electricity."[3]

As the primary speaker that morning, President George Q. Cannon reminded the Saints that despite all their political difficulties, which had been foreseen by Joseph Smith and Brigham Young, "God had kindly and generously given us the spirit of peace, and thrown around us so many things to cheer and comfort us in every trying time."[4] In concluding his address, President Cannon touched upon a subject that had direct relevance for Heber. Commenting on how Zion must take care of itself, he said, "Those who are gifted with business capacities must devote their talents to the general good the same as the Presidency, Apostles and leading Elders have done for the elevation and benefit of the masses. . . . We must not be influenced by selfish motives, but the talents and wealth and business ability must be utilized for the benefit of the whole community."[5] Even though his tenure as stake president had set back his business pursuits, Heber was surely one of the businessmen to whom President Cannon addressed himself. Elders Wilford Woodruff and Erastus Snow both spoke briefly before the morning session was adjourned until the afternoon. As President Grant would explain some years later, "I came to the Sunday afternoon meeting of the conference . . . with the assurance in my heart that Brother Teasdale and myself would be sustained as Apostles."[6]

Prophecies of His Calling

The incident with Brother Teasdale was not the first time Heber had been informed that he would become an Apostle as was his father, Jedediah M. Grant. As a young boy, Heber's mother often told him, "Heber, behave yourself and you will some day be an Apostle." Heber tried to dispel such notions, telling her that he had no interest in Church positions—that he only wanted to become a businessman. Yet his mother was not easily dissuaded. "Never mind," she would reply, "if you behave yourself you will be an Apostle."[7]

When Heber was only six, Rachel attended a Relief Society meeting in which Eliza R. Snow experienced the gift of tongues. After blessing several of those present, Eliza picked up the young Heber and likewise blessed him. As she had done with the other blessings, Zina D. Young interpreted, informing the boy and his mother that he would, one day, become an Apostle. There were others who acknowledged Heber's ecclesiastical future. Following dinner at Heber C. Kimball's home, the venerable Church leader picked up a very young Heber and placed him on the table. In talking to the boy, President Kimball characteristically began to prophesy. As Rachel later told her son,

> he prophesied that you should become one of the Apostles of the Lord Jesus Christ, and live to be a greater man in the Church than your own father; and that is the reason that I have told you that if you would behave yourself you would some day be an Apostle. I realized that if you did not behave yourself you never would attain to that position, no matter what you had been promised.[8]

Yet another witness of his apostolic calling came just after Heber had been made president of the Tooele stake. His six-month-old daughter, Lucy, became quite ill. With the child near death, President Grant sought out Brother Rowberry, the stake patriarch, to give her a blessing. Following the blessing, the patriarch turned to Heber and asked, "Did you get the witness of the spirit that your baby should live?" When he replied that he had not, Rowberry told him, "I did, and I know she is going to live." He then requested that Heber find some paper on which to record a patriarchal blessing for Lucy. A short time later when the two men met again, Rowberry approached his stake president: "Brother Grant, I want you to come to my office. I have a blessing in my heart for you of a Patriarchal nature." Heber complied, and the patriarch pronounced the blessing. He did not, however, give the complete blessing. As he subsequently told Heber, "I saw something that I dared not put in your blessing." Though the patriarch elaborated no further, Heber needed no explanation. Telling of this event years later, Heber explained, "I then had the impression (I was just twenty-four years of age when he made that remark and had not been made an Apostle) that I should live to preside over the Church."[9]

Call to the Twelve

When President Grant attended the Sunday afternoon session of conference, it was in great anticipation that the prophecies and promptings would be fulfilled—that though not quite twenty-six, he would become an Apostle. Charles Penrose began the meeting by reading the names of men called on missions since the previous conference. An additional sixty-nine names were then read off with these men being called to missions throughout Europe and the United States. President George Q. Cannon then got up to present the Church officers for a sustaining vote. He read the names of the First Presidency and the ten members of the Quorum of Twelve: Elders Wilford Woodruff, Charles C. Rich, Lorenzo Snow, Erastus Snow, Franklin D. Richards, Brigham Young Jr., Albert Carrington, Moses Thatcher, Francis M. Lyman, and John Henry Smith. Next the counselors to the Twelve, the Patriarch of the Church, the Presidents of the Seventy, the president of the Perpetual Emigration Fund and his assistants, the general architect and assistants, the auditing committee, as well as the conference clerk and Church reporter were all sustained. For Heber the sustainings must assuredly have dragged on. Then President Woodruff stood at the pulpit on behalf of the Twelve and Seventy and issued callings to Abraham H. Cannon and Theodore B. Lewis to the fill vacancies in the Quorum of the First Seven Presidents of Seventies. When President Woodruff was done, President John Taylor rose to give the concluding speech of the conference. Taylor did not issue any additional calls, and no mention was made of either Teasdale or Grant. Both men left the conference doubting the impression they had received.

Heber spent the week reprimanding himself for his egotism. However, on the following Friday, President John Taylor was at home in the Gardo House when he received a revelation. Directing Himself "to the Twelve, and to the Priesthood and people of my Church," the Lord announced that George Teasdale and Heber J. Grant were to be called to fill the vacancies so that the quorum might "be fully organized and prepared for the labors devolving upon" them.[10] President Taylor submitted the revelation to the Twelve for their approval, and it "was afterwards read to the Presidents of Stakes, First Presidents of Seventies and a few others."[11]

On Sunday the fifteenth, Heber received an unexpected telegram from his business partner, Nephi W. Clayton. It read: "You must be in Salt Lake tomorrow without fail." Despite the fact he had scheduled an appointment to deal with stake business in Tooele, he boarded the train and returned to Salt Lake. At the station he confronted Clayton regarding the message. His partner quickly replied that "it was not I who sent for you; it was Brother Lyman. He told me to send the telegram and sign my name to it. He told me to come and meet you and take you to the President's office. That is all I know."[12] Heber discovered the need for his return as the following day he met with the First Presidency and the Twelve. About this experience Heber reported:

> When I was called as one of the Apostles I arose to my feet to say it was beyond anything I was worthy of, and as I was rising the thought came to me, "You know as you know that you live that John Taylor is a prophet of God, and to decline this office when he had received a revelation is equivalent to repudiating the prophet." I said, "I will accept the office and do my best." I remember that it was with difficulty that I took my seat without fainting.[13]

In performing the ordination, President George Q. Cannon reiterated themes from his last conference talk as he issued a particularly pertinent warning to Heber—that he avoid "setting [his] mind on the things of this world."[14]

At the meeting's conclusion Heber approached George Teasdale, now Elder Teasdale, to complete the conversation they had started ten days earlier. Elder Grant told him, "I know what you were going to say to me on the sixth of October when you happened to choke half to death and then went into the meeting." When Elder Teasdale suggested that he could not possibly have known, Heber proceeded to complete the sentence that Teasdale had previously failed to finish: "You and I are going to be called to the apostleship." Somewhat surprised, Elder Teasdale explained, "That is what I was going to say, and then it occurred to me that I had no right to tell it, that I had received a manifestation from the Lord." Between the end of conference and his sustaining, Elder Teasdale "suffered the tortures of the damned for ten days, thinking I could not tell the difference between a manifestation from the Lord and one from the devil, that the devil had deceived me." Heber admitted to his fellow Apostle that in the intervening days, "I never prayed so hard in my life for anything as I did that the Lord would forgive me for the egotism of thinking that I was fit to be an Apostle, and that I was ready to go into that meeting ten days ago and vote for myself to be an Apostle."[15]

Less than a week later, Heber wrote his cousin Anthony W. Ivins, candidly commenting on his call. Apparently Heber was not the only one to anticipate his call, as he opened his letter by saying, "Well Tony, your predictions, made last March, as we were going to Saint George, that I would be one of the Apostles, has been fulfilled." He then went on to express his reservations at being qualified for such a position: "You know the true sentiments of my heart on this subject, (as well as many others) and that they were not in accord with your prediction, not that I feel to shrink from any duty, but because I did not, nor do I now, feel that my knowledge, ability, or testimony are of such a character as to entitle me to the position of an Apostle."[16]

Having associated with the leading men of the Church all his life, Heber had plenty of examples to follow. He told his cousin that

> Bro. Erastus Snow comes the nearest to my idea of what an Apostle should be of any member of the Twelve. When I recall his life and labors and stop to think how little time and attention he has for his family or his financial interests,

and how much time he has for the people and their interests, and how freely, and without a word of complaint, he
neglected his own comfort and worldly welfare for the
benefit of others, I am fully convinced that should I follow
his noble example, and I shall try to do so, that my financial interests are comparatively speaking at an end.

Though not completely ready to abandon his business dealings, he
did tell Anthony, "I have made up my mind that from this time forth
my life shall be devoted to the work of God upon the Earth. If He
gives me time to do my duties in His Kingdom and also make money,
all right; if not, all right. I feel in my heart to say 'Father, Thy will not
mine be done.'"[17]

In mid-November, Elder Grant received a congratulatory letter,
just as he had after his call as stake president, from his close friend
Richard W. Young, who was then in New York. Young indicated he
was not surprised at the call, only that "it is sooner than I looked for
it." Anticipating his friend's almost certain doubts, he sought to reas-
sure Heber:

As a young man, the youngest of the Quorum and as a
man without a very extensive experience in matters of
preaching, I can imagine that you feel impressed with your
unworthiness for the position, but let me give it you as my
frank opinion that the selection was one of the very best
that could be made, I have no desire to flatter you, but
simply to assist you in feeling more confidence in your
newly acquired dignity.

He extolled Heber for his "quickness to see a point" and honesty.
"Your conversation to me has always been as free from vapor and as
full of common sense, boiled down, as I have always been told your
father's was." He reminded Heber of the divine approbation reflected
in his call. "Fancy it," he went on to say, "God, the Good, the
Almighty ruler of the Universe, . . . He whom so many generations
have sought, . . . has been so far pleased with your integrity and
worth as to name you personally as one of His representatives on

Earth."[18] While attempting to build him up, Richard also acknowledged some of Heber's shortcomings: "My wish is that you may
devote yourself to study, for no adornment of the mind is unnecessary
to this work—that you may be blessed with the fullness of testimony
of God and His Work, . . . and that you may be deeply impressed
with the nature of your calling and become eminently useful therein
is my earnest prayer."[19]

Heber quickly wrote a reply to Richard, and as in the letter to
Ivins, he made clear his reservations about his abilities: "With refer-
ence to my new calling and my abilities to magnify the same, I must
say that I consider my position much in advance of my knowledge."
In comparing himself with several other members of the Twelve, he
openly acknowledged his deficiencies as a preacher.

> I regret very much that I have not a better knowledge of
> grammar, as I murder the "Queens English" most fear-
> fully—my orthography is perfectly *Emense* to say the
> least—I have not a good memory, or if I have it has been
> so badly neglected that I have not found out that it is
> good. My information on subjects relating to the advance-
> ment of a community amounts to nothing, I know little or
> nothing of History—and were it not that I have from
> fifteen to twenty-five years in which to study to overtake
> such men as Lyman, Joseph F. Smith, and others, and
> knowing that I have the right to call upon our Heavenly
> Father for assistance, I assure you that I should almost like
> backing out. A knowledge of grammar and orthography is
> necessary for a public speaker and one that has more or less
> writing to do. I naturally dislike both of these studies and
> have not much faith in becoming proficient in either.[20]

Though never one to back down from a challenge—having become
proficient in baseball and penmanship despite lacking natural
ability—Heber's doubts even led to some uncharacteristic pessimism.

Countering Young's praise, the new elder suggested, "Your inven-
tory of my abilities is 'way up.' I should like to have you get someone
to accept of your ideas but think it would be a difficult task, I may

have a little common sense—In fact I know that I have, I also know that my first ideas, impressions, or quickness to see a point whichever you see fit to call it, is not bad, but this really amounts to but very little when you are looking for a substantial leading man." Feeling that he had little to offer in terms of his current abilities, there was one idea that gave him comfort. "There is one thing that sustains me, however, and that is the fact that all powers, of mind or body, come from God and that He is perfectly able and willing to qualify me for His work provided I am faithful in doing my part—This I hope to be able to do faithfully—I am also pleased to know that I shall have the faith and confidence of the people—This is a great thing as I know from personal experience while laboring in Tooele County."[21]

The doubts about his call and abilities continued to plague Elder Grant throughout the initial months of his service. "From October [1882] when I was called to be one of the council of the Twelve, until the following February, I had but little joy and happiness in my labors." As he described it, "There was a spirit following me that told me that I lacked the experience, that I lacked the inspiration, that I lacked the testimony to be worthy of the position of an Apostle of the Lord Jesus Christ." Such was his admiration for previous members of the Twelve, so many of whom he knew personally, that he had diffi-culty envisioning himself worthy now to be a colleague. The adver-sary, he believed, took "advantage of that feeling in my heart, day and night, the spirit pursued me, suggesting that I resign, and when I testified of the divinity of the work we are engaged in, the words would come back, 'You haven't seen the Savior; you have no right to bear such a testimony.'"[22] This internal struggle left an "awful depres-sion upon me,"[23] a feeling that would remain even until his first missionary assignment as a member of the Twelve.

Elder Grant's First Mission

In the revelation that John Taylor received directing him to call Elders Teasdale and Grant, the Lord informed the leaders to "proceed forthwith and call to your aid any assistance that you may require from among the Seventies to assist you in your labors in introducing and maintaining the Gospel among the Lamanites throughout the land."[24] President Taylor wasted no time calling the newest Apostle to go on what would be Heber's first mission. But the internal battle raged on—the doubts were incessant. Truly he felt "oppressed." He was plagued with an "awful feeling of dread and doubt and with the suggestion hammering away at my brain that I ought to resign as an Apostle of the Lord Jesus Christ, that I had never done anything that entitled me to that distinction, that I had never performed any special labor, that I was not posted on the gospel, as an Apostle ought to be; that my mind had been given to the ordinary affairs of life, and that I should step aside and let some other man be called who, I believed, was better qualified for the position than myself."[25]

On 6 January 1883, Elder Grant joined Elder Brigham Young Jr., his companion for this and two more trips to Arizona in the coming months, on the 7:00 A.M. train leaving Ogden for Denver. Having never been away from his family for more than a couple of weeks, Heber had a hard time leaving them. In his journal he noted, "It was considerable of a task to say good-bye, knowing as I did that I should not see them again for six or seven months." His journal also indicated that Heber was aware of the danger such a mission entailed. He wrote, "I hope and pray that our lives may be spared so that we may again have the pleasure of meeting."[26] A little more than twenty-two years previous, George A. Smith Jr. was on a mission to the Moquis Indians, the same tribe Heber was to visit, when he was killed by Navajo Indians. Though he had not known the fallen missionary, Heber was acquainted with his parents, and this event clearly weighed on his mind as he made the trip.

From Denver the two men headed south to the San Luis Valley and the town of Manassa, where Mormons had settled four years earlier. Following their meetings they took a train to Durango, arriving the evening of 15 January. Expecting to be met in Durango, Heber and Brigham waited three days before finally hiring a team to continue on with their travels. Four miles out of Durango they met Luther C. Burnham, who was on his way to pick them up. That night the men stayed at Fort Lewis, and the temperature dropped to minus twenty-six degrees Fahrenheit. Heber awoke to "one of the coldest mornings that I ever experienced in my life. The wind was blowing and the thermometer was considerably below zero." Despite the cold, Heber, Brigham, and Brother Burnham planned to continue on as they were already several days behind schedule. The officers at the fort insisted, however, that the men wait until the weather improved. The Apostles and their companion waited but only until that afternoon. Before leaving, a Captain Daugherty loaned Heber a large buffalo overcoat that he could wear over his own coat. He later recalled that "but for this kindness on the part of the captain I am confident I would have greatly suffered from the cold, and notwithstanding the fact that I was very warmly clad independent of the captain's large buffalo overcoat, on several occasions I had to get out of the wagon and walk in order to keep warm." Noting that neither of his traveling companions seemed to be bothered by the cold as much, Heber wryly observed, "I supposed they escaped by not being so thin as I am."[27]

Their initial stop in Burnham, New Mexico, was little more than a day's travel. After a day of meetings on Monday 22 January, Brigham, Heber, and Brother Walter J. Stevens set out for Bluff City, Utah. Their hundred-mile wagon journey was hampered again by snowy weather. Setting up camp the first night on the banks of the San Juan River, the men built a large fire but found they could not warm themselves. That night they "retired and slept under so much bedding that the next morning we were tired from having held up so much weight." For half the trip, Elder Grant estimated, they traveled without knowing where the road was, "every little while getting out of the wagon to lift on the wheels to assist our team in getting through the snow-drift."[28] Arriving on Saturday afternoon, the two Apostles attended a YMMIA meeting that evening. Sunday and Monday were spent in additional meetings with the Saints. After visiting the members' farmland surrounding the fortlike dwelling, the three traveling companions climbed back into their wagon and left for Montezuma, where they held a meeting with Church members at William Hyde's home. Thursday found them on the road back to Burnham, a trip that Heber described as "scarcely as cold and unpleasant as when we made the trip from Burnham to Bluff."[29]

Returning the same way they had come, the Apostles traveled to Durango where they caught a train that took them right to the town of Manassa. It was back at Silas Smith's home that the men finally received news from home. As Heber later commented, "Thirty-three days from home, and no letters gives a person a very good appetite for home news, and we enjoyed the contents of our mail very much."[30] Gone over a month, the men had yet to begin their mission to the Native Americans.

Arizona, the Native Americans, and a "Remarkable Visitation"

The trip to Arizona required that the Apostles first travel into New Mexico, a journey punctuated by miserable sleeping accommodations and poor travel arrangements. Taking the train to the end of its line, Elders Young and Grant arrived in the "miserable little town" of Espanola. There they made the mistake of choosing lodging with a saloon next door. Along with having a "miserable bed," the two missionaries were "kept awake nearly all night by the yelling and shooting carried on by some of the men freely patronizing" the saloon.[31]

After a bad night's sleep, they had a worse trip to Santa Fe. Unable to travel by train, they hired a local man with a wagon and mules. The twenty-three-mile journey lasted all day and into the evening. They would have arrived even later if Heber "had not got permission from the Mexican to exercise my right arm in mauling his mules." To give an idea just how slow they went, Heber explained that "for some eight to ten miles four burros loaded with corn fodder kept from one to twenty rods ahead of us, and I doubt we would have been able to pass them but for the fact that one of them fell down and could not get up until part of his load was removed, which gave us a slight lead." From Santa Fe it was on to Albuquerque where they stayed in the Palace Hotel, a modern building with a "great deal of style." Always quick to assess financial situations, Heber did note that the hotel was run on an "economical scale," suggesting that "it was not a good paying investment, and that it was many years in advance of the needs of the city." Despite the fine accommodations, Heber didn't sleep any better than in Espanola. A billiard room was located beneath their room, and Heber found that the "the racket kept up during the night was almost unbearable."[32]

Their travels eventually took them to President Lot Smith's home in Sunset, Arizona, where they arrived on 16 February. It was only after his arrival in Arizona that Elder Grant received a letter from his mother indicating that his third daughter, Florence, had been born.

The Apostles held meetings with Saints in Sunset and Tuba City before setting off for the seven villages of the Moquis Indians and their planned proselytizing. One evening their party, which included Lot Smith and a dozen or so other men, camped near "George A. Spring." Having taken "a deep interest in visiting the lonely spot where the young man had met his death," Heber volunteered to take the animals there to be watered.[33]

As they continued traveling the next day, Heber was riding a small mule alongside Lot Smith, who was on horseback. Lagging some distance behind the other riders and wagons, Heber noticed a diverging trail. Inquiring of Smith, he discovered that following the trail would enable him to bypass the lengthy detour they were to take as the wagons could not get over the rough terrain. Wanting to be alone for a time, he told Smith that he would meet up with the party where the trail and road converged.

A mile or so into his solo travels, Heber received a powerful witness of his calling. In what he described as "one of the most real things in all my life," he listened in on a conversation of his father, the Prophet Joseph Smith, and the Savior. So real was the event that Heber "seemed to hear the words that were spoken." Listening with a "great deal of interest," he heard them converse about the status of the Quorum of the Twelve following the previous October conference. They addressed "the question that a mistake had been made in not filling those two vacancies and that in all probability it would be another six months before the Quorum would be completed." Discussing who they thought ought to fill the positions, they agreed that a revelation needed to be sent in order to correct the mistake. Heber reported:

> It was given to me that the Prophet Joseph Smith and my father mentioned me and requested that I be called to that position. I sat there and wept for joy. It was given to me that I had done nothing to entitle me to that exalted position, except that I had lived a clean, sweet life. It was given to me that because of my father's having practically sacrificed his life in what was known as the great reformation, so to speak, of the people in early days, having been

practically a martyr, that the Prophet Joseph and my
father desired me to have that position, and it was
because of their faithful labors that I was called, and not
because of anything I had done of myself or any great
thing that I had accomplished.[34]

Following this revelation, the depression and "awful dread" that
Heber had felt since his call finally dissipated. Though he had not
"earned" his calling, the call nonetheless had come from the Savior at
the suggestion of his father and Joseph Smith. And with this revelation, he could finally preach in confidence.

On 6 March the two Apostles and their party arrived at the first
Moquis village, which was located on a hill seven hundred feet above
the surrounding valley. The men visited the Indians' homes and
toured their village. Heber, in describing this visit to readers of the
Contributor magazine, was at times quite judgmental. He suggested
that the narrow streets in the village were "the most filthy and dirty
alleys through which I ever passed."[35] When offered what he called
"pica" bread, paper-thin bread baked on a stone, he refused on
account of the filthy conditions in which the bread was prepared.
Later in the trip he refused an offer of pudding because "the manner
of brewing the yeast [young girls chewed the cornmeal] seemed to
have entirely destroyed my appetite, as well as my curiosity, to
discover the taste of the Moquis pudding." While all the villages were
located on large prominences, some as high as 1,200 feet, and
comprised the same adobe houses, Heber acknowledged that all were
not as dirty as the first. Nonetheless, his visit to each of the villages,
"gave me anything but a favorable impression."[36]

The men met with little success in preaching the gospel. In a letter
to his wife, Elder Grant wrote, "The inhabitants with some few exceptions were perfectly indifferent as to what we had to say." He did
acknowledge that "some listened with marked attention and promised
to follow our advice" on the need to be honest, to stop stealing, and to
clean up their villages. They were not able to preach "the principles of
the gospel on account of the inability of the inhabitants to understand
or comprehend the meaning of them."[37] The gospel instruction was
saved for the subsequent visits to the Arizona Saints.

Their visit to the reservation concluded with a conversation with Manuelito, a Navajo chief. Although he could not understand "a word he said," Elder Grant later recalled that the chief "spoke with a fire and a force and fervor that I had seldom heard in all my life."[38] Their interpreter, Brother Ernest Titjen, believed the speech was the most eloquent he had ever heard, and "he regretted very much that we did not understand the Navajo language so that we could have appreciated Manuelito's eloquence."[39] The chief discussed the wrongs his tribe had suffered, indicating that whites, "except only the 'Mormons,'" had treated them unjustly. Despite troubles in that portion of the reservation, Manuelito told them, "You are absolutely safe to travel among the Navajos, because I will send word ahead that you are 'Mormons,' and they know that 'Mormons' are the friends of the red men."[40] The chief agreed to welcome Mormon missionaries if they were sent, and they bid adieu. The "friends" passed through the territory without incident and returned to Lot Smith's home in Sunset.

The next thirty days of their mission Brigham and Heber spent visiting the Saints in St. Joseph, Woodruff, Snowflake, Taylorsville, Erastus, Omer, St. Johns, and other towns. A conference of the Snowflake stake was held at the end of March, and missionaries from the stake, as well as others in other towns, were called to preach to the Native Americans on the Little Colorado.

The weather continued to hamper their travels. During a trip to the Zuni village on the Navajo reservation, a sandstorm made it difficult to see where they were going. The wind, Heber noted on 13 April, "kept up a gale all night." Sleeping in a wagon, the elders found out that sleep was "hard work instead of rest," and their condition was exacerbated by the snowfall that evening. Days later Elder Brigham Young Jr. fell ill with a fever, and he was "suffering considerable with rheumatism in his shoulders." Talk of returning home soon began among the men. Of this prospect, Heber was quite hesitant, not wanting to terminate the mission prematurely. In his journal he wrote: "I have stated from the first that to consult my own feelings I would say go on and carry out our program and visit southern Arizona. I finally concluded that all of the brethren thought it best for us to return, and I said, 'Let's go home.' Although my business needs me and I will be delighted to go home, I must say that I dislike starting before our program has been completed."[41] With the decision made, the men quickly made their way home, arriving on Monday, 23 April 1883.

Return Trips to Arizona

Earning the self-appointed moniker the "Arizona Apostle," Elder Grant made two additional journeys to Arizona before the end of 1884. Following the October 1883 conference Heber prepared once again to leave, and on the twenty-ninth he boarded another train for Denver where he was to meet his companions: Brigham Young Jr. and Young's wife and daughter. As with the previous mission, Heber must have had some concerns about this assignment. Before leaving he wrote in his journal: "This morning I arranged with my partners, Goddard and Wells, that in case of my death they were to continue the business of our firm and pay one half the profit to my wife, Lucy, until such time as they saw fit to purchase my interest for $4,000."[42] The two-month mission largely consisted of visiting Church members, checking on the missionaries sent to the Native Americans, and appointing new elders for the work. While he certainly must have tried to complete his work before 25 December, he spent the entire Christmas day traveling from Espanola to Manassa. After several days of meetings in the small town, Heber was able to make it home in time for New Year's.

In 1884 President John Taylor again assigned Elders Young and Grant to visit the Arizona settlements, which they did for most of November. President Taylor had also directed them "to choose a party of competent men and proceed into Mexico." As Heber explained, "Our trip into Sonora, Mexico, is for the purpose of visiting the Chief of the Yaqui Indian nation and to try to find a place on the upper Yaqui for a settlement, . . . a place for a city of refuge."[43] It was a trip that would justify his earlier concerns of ever seeing his family again as they had to travel through a land plagued by yellow fever to visit the Yaqui Indians, who were in open rebellion against the Mexican government.

Rendezvousing in Nogales, Arizona, their traveling party consisted of twenty-five men, five wagons, three carriages, and a total of thirty-two animals. After a several-hour delay at the border, Heber wrote, "For the first time in my life I put my foot on soil of a foreign country."[44] Circumventing the small towns they passed—they had been warned previously of the pervading illness—they enjoyed the countryside. On 30 November the party left camp at 6:30 A.M. and traveled nine miles before stopping for water. In a journal entry reminiscent of his previous missions, Heber wrote: "We watered our animals from one of the most filthy tanks I ever saw. It was this or nothing. We had to pay for the water, five cents per animal. Some of our party drank from the tank but I did not care to do so although I was quite thirsty. The water looked like it had been there all summer at least. Animals were driven into it, and it looked more like the remains of a cow yard than a tank saved for the use of animals and man."[45] Though Heber had claimed he had been "hardened" by his camping experiences,[46] his sensibilities had not been completely dulled, and he preferred to go without.

Each night guards were posted around camp to protect the men and their animals. For additional protection, Brigham Young Jr. suggested that they "hold occasional meetings and call upon the Lord." Apparently, Heber said, "he felt that we would be more apt to fully accomplish our mission if we were prayerful and went trusting in our Heavenly Father."[47] After arriving in Hermosillo safely, Brigham and Heber met with the governor of Sonora. While he was quite pleasant with the Apostles, the governor reiterated what they had already heard numerous times. Heber said, "We have been warned by every Mexican official that we have met from the consul at Tucson to the secretary in Sonora not to go into the country on the Yaqui River occupied by the Yaqui Indians. The secretary informed us that the Yaquis would take our arms and animals and that we would be fortunate if we escaped with our lives." This threat was repeated to Brigham and the six men accompanying him on 7 December. While they boarded a boat to take them up the Yaqui River, a group of Mexicans and Yaquis gathered and "told the party to confess their sins as they would not come back alive."[48]

Heber's experience at their camp just outside Hermosillo was certainly less eventful, and he found it "a tiresome task to be lying in a camp doing nothing." Yet the men waited, passing the time reading and feasting on oranges. When Brigham's group returned on the fourteenth, Heber saw that all were alive but not all well. Brigham had come down with yellow fever, and Heber "felt impressed that he [Young] must not do any traveling by team." The Apostles departed Hermosillo the next day by train and arrived in Salt Lake three days later.

When Brigham's party visited the Yaqui, the Indians were anxious to have missionaries come teach them more about the Book of Mormon, and they were quite willing to provide land for a Mormon settlement. After Heber and Brigham's return to Utah, however, the American press began reporting "the particulars of an agreement said to have been made between the Mormons and the Indians by which war on the Mexican government was to be conducted by their united forces."[49] The fallout from these reports eventually necessitated that the Church desist in proselytizing to the Yaquis and seeking a refuge on their lands.

As a junior Apostle, Heber willingly accepted the repeated calls to visit the Saints in Arizona and Mexico.[50] He felt it was his duty to endure the hardships of these lengthy journeys, which contrasted with the amenities Heber enjoyed at home. "However hard the way," his daughter Rachel wrote, "the joyful welcome at each branch or ward, the happy hours spent in hospitable homes, the mingling of congenial spirits in humble worship richly compensated for the physical hardships entailed by such travel."[51]

NOTES TO CHAPTER 3

1. *JD*, 22:37.
2. *JD*, 22:38.
3. CR, October 1922, 2.
4. "Fifty-Second Semi-annual Conference," *MS*, 20 November 1882, 739.
5. Ibid., 740.
6. CR, October 1922, 2.
7. CR, April 1935, 13.
8. Ibid., 14.
9. Heber J. Grant, "The 'Still Small Voice,'" *IE*, December 1938, 712.

10. James R. Clark, comp. *Messages of the First Presidency of The Church of Jesus Christ of Latter-day Saints*, 6 vols. (Salt Lake City: Bookcraft, 1965), 2:348.

11. "Correspondence," *MS*, 13 November 1882, 732.

12. CR, October 1942, 25.

13. CR, April 1941, 4.

14. Ronald W. Walker, "Young Heber J. Grant and His Call to the Apostleship," *BYU Studies* 18 (fall 1977): 123.

15. CR, October 1942, 25.

16. Grant, "The President's Thoughts on His Call to Apostleship," *IE*, November 1938, 650.

17. Ibid.

18. Walker, "Young Heber J. Grant and His Call to the Apostleship," 124.

19. Ibid., 125.

20. Ibid., 125; emphasis in original.

21. Ibid., 125–26.

22. CR, October 1918, 23. Grant later wrote of this experience, stating the following: "When I would testify of my knowledge that Jesus is the Christ, the Son of the living God, the Redeemer of mankind, it seemed as though a voice would say to me: 'You lie! You lie! You have never seen Him.'" Grant, "President Grant's Opening Conference Message," *IE*, May 1941, 267.

23. CR, October 1919, 125.

24. Clark, *Messages of the First Presidency*, 2:348.

25. CR, October 1919, 125.

26. Rachel Grant Taylor, "The Arizona Apostle," *IE*, July 1942, 432.

27. Grant, "Visit to the Moquis," *Contributor*, January 1896, 154.

28. Ibid., 155.

29. Ibid., 156.

30. Ibid.

31. Grant, "Visit to the Moquis," *Contributor*, February 1896, 203.

32. Ibid.

33. Ibid., 205.

34. CR, April 1941, 5.

35. Grant, "Visit to the Moquis," *Contributor*, February 1896, 206.

36. Grant, "Visit to the Moquis," *Contributor*, April 1896, 332.

37. Taylor, "The Arizona Apostle," 475–76.

38. CR, October 1919, 124.

39. Grant, "Visit to the Moquis," *Contributor,* April 1896, 334.

40. CR, October 1919, 124.

41. Taylor, "The Arizona Apostle," 477.

42. Ibid.

43. Grant, "Journey to Mexico—1884," comp. Rachel Grant Taylor, *IE,* November 1942, 696.

44. Ibid.

45. Ibid., 697.

46. Grant, "Visit to the Moquis," *Contributor,* April 1896, 331.

47. Grant, "Journey to Mexico—1884," 697.

48. Ibid., 697–98.

49. Ibid., 698.

50. John A. Widtsoe, "President Grant the Man," *IE,* November 1936, 663.

51. Taylor, "The Arizona Apostle," 432.

~ FOUR ~

Heber J. Grant's most intimate and influential associations were with the women in his life. Raised by his widowed mother, Heber married three times, and his wives bore him ten daughters and two sons. Neither son, however, lived past childhood. Though these losses saddened Heber, they didn't make him resentful of his living daughters. He treasured each one and eagerly anticipated reuniting with them after long separations. In addition to the teaching he offered at home, Heber provided his daughters with fine training and education. He was always proud of their accomplishments and was also thrilled when many became outstanding leaders in the Church.

Lucy and Heber Sealed in the St. George Temple

Heber's devotion to his family was evident in his strong desire to be sealed to them for time and all eternity in a temple of the Lord. At twenty, he asked Lucy Stringham, then a nineteen-year-old school-teacher, to be his wife. As the nearby Salt Lake Temple was not yet completed, many of Lucy and Heber's friends recommended that they marry civilly and wait until the temple in Salt Lake was completed to be sealed with whatever children they had. Lucy and Heber, however, were determined to be married in the Lord's temple from the start.

In order to be married in the temple, Heber and Lucy had to make the journey to St. George. In October 1877 they boarded a train in Salt Lake that took them south to Utah County. From Santaquin, Utah, they endured a seven-day wagon trip that took them over "unimproved and uncertain roads."[1] The couple traveled with Apostle Erastus Snow, and at night they stayed in the homes of

Saints who lived along the way. These nightly visits were an added source of delight for Heber. "I met a great many people who expressed pleasure at entertaining me as a son of Jedediah M. Grant. I do not recall in the same length of time that I ever heard so many kind expressions regarding my father as I did on that trip."[2] In St. George, the couple stayed at Elder Snow's home, and it was he who married them on 1 November 1877.

Years later, one of the Grant daughters, speaking on behalf of the Young Women's General Board, said, "I am very grateful to the Lord that I was properly born, born under the covenant, born of parents that had been properly married and sealed in the temple of the Lord." Heber said that when he heard this, "Tears came into my eyes, because her mother died before the Salt Lake Temple was completed, and I was grateful that I had not listened to the remarks of my friends who had tried to persuade me not to go to the St. George Temple to be married. I was very grateful for the inspiration and determination I had to start life right."[3]

The family of Heber and Lucy Stringham Grant.

With the right beginning to their marriage, Heber and Lucy lived together very happily. Lucy was a striking, beautiful woman who dedicated her short married life to her family. Her daughters remembered her fondly, writing verses and prose to praise and honor her. Her second daughter and namesake recalled her mother's spiritual sensitivities: "A young boy who came to stay at our home when Father was away has told us about Mother's fervent prayers. He said those prayers had a deep influence for good upon his life."[4]

During Lucy and Heber's time together, money and material means were had in abundance. Heber loved to use his financial success to bless his family, and there were men and women hired to look after things around the house and stables. Despite the hired help, Lucy never allowed her children to be taken care of by another. Her schoolteacher training clearly influenced her excellent mothering as later her children recalled gathering round her to be read to and taught.[5]

After growing up in poverty, Lucy appreciated the material blessings with which Heber provided her. "Mother appreciated everything she had," recalled her second daughter. "After so many years of poverty, to have an abundance, and being able to help her brothers and sisters, and to give some of them a home, and to add to their happiness was a great joy to her. I believe one of the greatest pleasures of Father's life was doing nice things for his wives and family. He showered them with gifts. Mother had lovely jewelry, fine clothes, beautiful furniture and pictures in the home."[6] One such piece of furniture was a Steinway piano that Heber purchased. He paid for lessons for his daughters so they could play for him when he requested. With fondness, Lutie and Rachel remembered having their mother tie their hair up in rags to curl it before they performed for the company so often entertained in the Grant household.[7]

Augusta and Emily

As a member of the Twelve in the 1880s, Heber was expected to practice plural marriage. Political conditions of the time, however, were such that many practitioners of plural marriage had to live "on the underground," keeping their marriages secret and rarely seeing their spouses in order to evade imprisonment. Fully aware of these difficulties, three years after becoming an Apostle, at the age of twenty-eight, Heber married his second and third wives, Augusta Winters and Emily Harris Wells. On 20 February 1884, Augusta wrote in her journal: "A day long to be remembered. This evening I gave my decision in a matter that I have been considering for a long time. I feel that I have decided wisely and well. I cannot say even here what I would like to." Then on the day she married Heber, 26 May 1884, Augusta observed in her journal: "The most eventful day of my life!"[8] The next day, 27 May, Heber married Emily Harris Wells. Emily's oldest daughter, Dessie, said: "She was married with the consent and approval of Lucy, Father's first wife. Mother and Aunt Lucy had grown up in the same community and had been friends for many years. On the other hand Mother had met Augusta Winters Grant, Father's second wife, only a few times before her marriage."[9] Heber's first wife, Lucy, gave her consent to these unions, and later in life she expressed profound love and gratitude for Heber's other wives.

After Augusta married Heber, her life didn't change significantly as she could not disclose her marriage; she continued to teach school, while Heber lived with Lucy. But life "on the underground" was anything but easy for the newlywed wife. On 2 September 1884, she wrote in her journal: "Attended conference here [Provo, Utah] in the afternoon. Saw Apostle Francis M. Lyman. I am glad to see him because he reminds me of *someone else* whom I cannot see or even *mention*. I cried and cried after I had gone to bed. . . . I am afraid I felt rather rebellious for a time, but I got over it."[10] Even though these years of living apart from Heber were clearly difficult, Augusta was filled with faith. She recorded that during the Christmas season Heber wrote "a letter nearly every day full of loving words and wishes and prayers for my . . . happiness."[11]

Augusta was able use this time to prepare her mind for her later position as wife of the President of the Church. She studied French with Dr. James E. Talmage at Brigham Young University, then known as Timpanogos Academy. Through teaching and then going to school, then teaching again when her funds were exhausted, Augusta became one of the few women at the time to earn an advanced degree. She graduated from the University of Utah in 1887.[12]

Emily also lived on the underground with an assumed name, and when she had been married a year she sailed to England to live for a time with her father, Daniel H. Wells, who was serving as president of the European mission. Soon after her arrival there her first child was born in the mission home in Liverpool. Like Augusta, Emily also took advantage of the opportunity she now had to improve her mind.

She loved to travel, and she attended concerts and plays and visited the birthplaces and homes of such greats as Shakespeare, Scott, Burns, and Moore. She became a connoisseur of silver, fine china, and antiques. Emily was sustained by kind and loving letters that came to her on a consistent basis from her husband.[13]

After five years of living a secret life as the wife of Heber J. Grant, Augusta became pregnant with his child. This pregnancy forced her into hiding, where she suffered loneliness while awaiting the birth of her child, despite the caring and consistent letters she received from her husband. She explained:

> There has been a great change in my life. I am truly "on the underground." Though I do not wish to complain and am deeply thankful for the cause that led me here, yet many things are trying in the extreme. . . . Though I have a comfortable place to stay, the thought that I am virtually a prisoner makes me very sad, and I spend many hours in tears. I often go out for a walk when night comes, and sometimes I walk past Delia's home and can look in the brightly lighted windows and see them all with some of my friends from home. The thought that I cannot go into my own sister's home but must stay outside in the darkness nearly breaks my heart. . . . If I could only go about and live like other people, I would be *so happy.* I have received many tokens of my dear husband's love and kindness, though to think that he cannot always see me when he is in the same town seems cruel. Everyone says, "It isn't wise, it isn't wise," until I wish there were no such word as "wise" in the English language! . . . I am in the hands of the Lord, and I have perfect confidence in him that all will be well with me. I am thankful to him for my dear husband and his love.[14]

Not long after the birth of her only child, Mary, Augusta moved to New England, living under an assumed name. Eventually she found her way to New York, where she lived pleasantly under Heber's financial protection. Being a successful businessman of considerable means, Heber never hesitated to send Augusta tickets for concerts or plays or anything that would please her. He also sent his friends to visit her in her exile and make her life pleasant. During this time, while raising her young daughter, Augusta became a gracious host to a multitude of her husband's friends.

The highlights of her life were occasional visits from her husband when he was traveling on behalf of the Church or his businesses. On one of these visits Heber brought Lucy and introduced her for the first time to Augusta; it was the only time the two ever met. Augusta found Lucy to be even more pleasant than she had anticipated. Throughout the brief visit, the family attended theaters and plays, but they also found time to shop together. Heber was always willing to spend money for the pleasure of others, especially his family. Lucy bought many lovely things and insisted that Augusta have all of the same opportunities to shop that she had. Finally, the highlight of the whole trip was when Heber, ever fair and kind, bought a sealskin coat for each wife. Augusta was so thrilled she could hardly sleep that night.

The women in New York were not the only ones to receive the privilege of the coat. Emily also received gifts from the big city. Her daughter Dessie recalled this event as her earliest memory of her father:

> The first Christmas I can remember, we were living in Southern Colorado, many miles from the railroad. It was difficult to send things there, and, I suppose, very expensive. But one day, shortly before Christmas, a wagon stopped in front of our house. An event, did you say? Mother said she saw only two strange wagons all the time we lived there, and this was one of them. A man got out of the wagon and began unloading boxes, sacks, barrels, and packages. There were oranges and bananas—great delicacies for that place,—there were apples and candy, nuts and raisins. There were lovely dolls and toys and new dresses and a *sealskin* coat for mother. The most thrilling things imaginable! This arrival of gifts from Father not only changed our Christmas but that of all the people in the little town, for they were all invited to share with us.[15]

At the conclusion of Lucy and Heber's trip to New York, Lucy reportedly proclaimed, "I love Augusta."[16] Perhaps through being married to the same man, perhaps through their faith, or perhaps through other means, these two women had, in one meeting, created a relationship that was to last beyond the bounds of life itself. Augusta eventually returned to Utah, where she was happily received at her parent's home in Pleasant Grove, Utah. She then had the happy opportunity to travel with her husband on a couple of occasions. About one of these trips, in 1891, Augusta wrote in her journal: "I have now to record one of the most delightful trips of my life with my dear husband. . . . We spent several days pleasantly in Portland, the last a quiet, happy Sunday, walking about the parks and reading. Heber is reading aloud to me Victor Hugo's *Les Miserables.*"[17]

Yet despite these happy moments, many wives in plural marriages at times felt unneeded, and Augusta was no exception. "There seems to be no place where I am needed. I am just a care that must be disposed of some way. But how? The one thing that I have dreamed of and longed for is my precious baby, and I thank God with all my heart for her, and pray earnestly that I may be worthy of her and all other blessings the Lord may have in store for me. If I am rebellious, oh Lord, forgive me, and help me to be humble, to submit to thy will in all things, for I know not which way to turn, and thou alone knowest what is in store for all of us in the future."[18] Doubtless each of the women in Heber's family had to find a great deal of humility and trust that the Lord would take care of their future.

The Passing of Lucy Grant

Augusta's life changed dramatically with the death of Heber's first wife Lucy. Lucy had become ill just after she and Heber had moved to Tooele in 1881, and her "stomach and female troubles," as her daughter Lucy described her illness, became debilitating a decade later when she was in her early thirties. Having given birth to five daughters—Rachel, Lucy, Florence, Edith, and Anna—Lucy finally gave birth to a son Heber. However, as her daughter reported, Lucy was never well after the birth of her son, and she "was on the couch a good part of the time."[19] Lucy spent her remaining years sick, which included a lengthy stay at St. Mary's Hospital in San Francisco.

While Lucy received treatment in the California hospital, Heber visited when he could, and he wrote her daily. "Almost every day," a daughter noted, "a letter reached her, and if for some reason it was delayed even the nurses would notice it." The sister superior at the Catholic hospital was most impressed with Heber's displays of kindness and love, and she told Lucy that "in all her years of nursing she had never had any man treat his wife as considerately as [she] was treated."[20]

Heber was just as attentive to Lucy when they were at home. "Father was Mother's nurse," reported his daughter Lucy. "He seldom left home except for his meetings. . . . No person could have been more considerate, more tender, than Father."[21] In his journal Heber noted the progression of his wife's illness. On 23 November 1892 he wrote, "I have shed some bitter tears this afternoon as Lucy feels that she cannot get well and she suffers so much she has little desire to recover. She has eaten almost nothing for nearly two weeks."[22] Although Heber did not think she had stomach cancer, the last three months of her illness were particularly difficult as Lucy was unable to keep food down. It was her daughter's assessment that Lucy "literally starved to death."[23] As the weeks passed and the disease worsened, Heber and Lucy spoke of their future apart, and they "both shed tears at our contemplated separation."[24]

One hour before Lucy's death, on 3 January 1893, Heber called their six children into her room to tell them their mother was dying. Lutie, his twelve-year-old daughter responded, "Papa, I do not want my mamma to die. I have been with you in the hospital in San Francisco for six months; time and time again when mamma was in distress you had administered to her and she has been relieved of her pain and quietly gone to sleep. I want you to lay hands upon my mamma and heal her." Despite his daughter's plea, Heber recalled, "I was thoroughly convinced in my own mind and in my own heart, when my first wife left me by death, that it was the will of the Lord that she should be called away. I bowed in humility at her death." He told as much to his daughter and sent her out of the room.

> I then knelt down by the bed of my wife (who by this time
> had lost consciousness) and I told the Lord I acknowledged
> His hand in life, in death, in joy, in sorrow, in prosperity,

or adversity. I thanked Him for the knowledge I had that my wife belonged to me for all eternity, that the gospel of Jesus Christ had been restored, that I knew that by the power and authority of the Priesthood here on the earth that I could and would have my wife forever if I were only faithful as she had been. But I told the Lord that I lacked the strength to have my wife die and to have it affect the faith of my little children in the ordinances of the gospel of Jesus Christ; and I supplicated the Lord with all the strength that I possessed, that He would give to that little girl of mine a knowledge that it was His mind and His will that her mamma should die.

Soon after, Lucy died with Heber beside her. Even with the assurances he felt, the moment must have been a sorrowful one when Heber called his children into the room to report their mother's death. Lucy's only son, who carried his father's name, was six years of age and was weeping bitterly when Lutie, calm as could be, wrapped her arms around him and said, "Do not weep, do not cry, Heber; since we went out of this room the voice of the Lord from heaven has said to me, 'In the death of your mamma the will of the Lord shall be done.'"[25] Lucy had suffered a great deal; however, till the end she was loving and gracious to Heber's other wives, thinking of her family and what was best for them. Both her oldest daughter, Rachel, and Heber reported that Lucy's last words to her husband were, "I can die peacefully because a woman that I love and that you love is to rear my five little girls and my baby boy."[26]

When Augusta did enter the household to take Lucy's place, she recorded, "There was no dark and mournful spirit in that home when I entered it, but rather a feeling of calm and peace."[27] The peace that surrounded Heber in his home life, even when he was afflicted by great adversity and tragedy, surely influenced him and enabled him to better serve as a leader in the Church.

More Illness in the Family

After Lucy's death, Heber took his three oldest daughters on a trip to the East Coast in order to help them forget some of the pain and grief they were feeling. While they were in Washington, D.C., Rachel, the oldest daughter, contracted diphtheria, which was near to a death sentence and was extremely contagious. Lutie, his second daughter, soon also got the disease. Away from home, suffering under the grief of Lucy's death, Heber felt a burden nearly too great to bear. His agony at the thought of the possible death of his daughters was surely overwhelming, but he remained the ever-vigilant father.

> I heard the doctor say to the nurse regarding my second daughter, "If you miss giving that child a stimulant every fifteen minutes—if you miss just once—she will die. She cannot live a half hour without this stimulant." I stayed up all night to see that she did not miss giving the stimulant, and the next morning the child was no better. I went into my room and shed some bitter tears at the thought that, in all probability, I should have to take that little girl home in a coffin. Kneeling down, I pleaded with the Lord to spare her life, for the very joy I was giving to my girls added to and intensified my own sorrow; and I asked that I be not obliged to have an additional sorrow in taking that little girl, whom I had brought away from home to give her pleasure in order that she might forget the death of her mamma, back to her home in a coffin. I begged that that might not come into my life. The testimony of the Spirit came to me: "The power of the Priesthood is here on the earth. Send for the elders and rebuke the power of the destroyer and that girl shall live."

As George Q. Cannon was visiting in Washington at the time, Heber sent for his fellow Apostle. Elder Cannon came immediately, and he and Hiram B. Clawson pronounced the blessing. In confirming the anointing, Elder Cannon announced, "'The adversary, the destroyer, has decreed your death and made public announcement of his decree, but by the authority of the Priesthood of God which we hold as His servants, and in the name of Jesus Christ, our Redeemer, we rebuke the decree of the destroyer and say, you shall live.'"[28]

Although two trained nurses were brought in to care for his daughters, Heber remained attentive throughout their recovery, "scarcely [leaving] the room night and day." As the girls improved, he read aloud to them hour after hour. Concerning her convalescence, Lutie recalled that her father "brought me presents and dainties as I was able to enjoy them and in the most wonderful way did as much as the fondest mother could."[29] After the children had recovered enough to travel home and the family was about to leave, the man who owned the boarding house where they had been staying approached Heber. He said that his wife believed in spiritualistic mediums, and when the children were taken ill she went to see one of these mediums. The medium said, "'I see in your home two little girls; I see that the older one of the two little girls is taken sick. I see that she is very sick. I now see that the next little girl is taken sick. I now see that she is very sick. I now see that both of them are sick nigh unto death. I now see the older of the two girls recover. I now see the second little girl die.' She then described the body passing in a coffin from Washington to Salt Lake," describing the Salt Lake Valley as "almost completely surrounded by mountains," and a burial site "on the side hills."[30] Upon hearing this account, Heber finally recognized the significance of Cannon's rebuke of the destroyer. The children and their father arrived home just in time to attend the first session of the Salt Lake Temple dedication. Though other children in the Grant home contracted diphtheria shortly thereafter, all survived.[31]

Meager Times

Lucy and Heber's six children were left to Augusta's care. She was happy with her new situation as the mother of many children, even though it brought with it its own challenges. "I feel that the Lord has blessed me thus far. The children are just as lovely to me as they can be, and, with the continued blessings of the Lord, I trust I may retain their love, and that we may be a united and happy family. If this can only be the case I shall feel fully repaid for any extra cares I may have."[32] Augusta had never before taken care of a home, so she relied heavily on Heber's mother and the oldest girls, who loved to cook and help around the house. Yet Augusta had an orderly mind and was a good manager of the household.

Augusta Winters Grant,
Heber's second wife.

Home life at the Grants following the panic of 1893 was one of limited means. Each member of the family contributed by earning and saving money, and none of the children complained about the necessary measures taken to cut back on expenses. Heber wrote a letter to a friend during this time describing and admiring Augusta's frugality and efficiency as the manager of their home. "She fed and partially clothed a family of ten with the *enormous* amount of seventy-five dollars a month! And part of the amount was tithing office scrip. When the children asked for a second glass of milk, they couldn't have it, because we couldn't afford that much milk. Meat was quite a scarcity in our home. She [never] made out one word of complaint, although she had at one time been drawing a salary of considerably more than the allowance on which she had to take care of the family."[33]

The children remembered their life at 14 Second East Street as a happy time, despite being poor. They learned to earn money to contribute to the Sunday School fund, to pay their tithing, and to work hard. They also enjoyed their associations with each other and with their family. One daughter fondly recalled helping Grandma Grant with the prominent featherbed in her upstairs room. It had to be aired out each day for an hour or two, and it wasn't uncommon for Rachel to solicit the help of her granddaughters in this difficult task. In the evening the family would often sit around the fire in the parlor and read together or listen to their father read to them. Heber, who always enjoyed listening to others sing, loved to sit and listen to his daughters play the Steinway piano and sing hymns. The home was well loved and well lived in.[34]

During this time, Augusta continued to expand her mind. She worked to establish a free kindergarten, organized the "author's club" for women who desired to study great authors and their works, and continued to read for her own enjoyment. When Heber was home they resolved to read twenty pages a day together from a religious work, though it was difficult to find time to complete it. They read from the scriptures and from Elder Talmage's works. Augusta read every night a little after the others had gone to bed. She read Homer and studied shorthand and French. She also gave a great deal of attention to Church callings. Asked to serve on the General Board of the Young Ladies Mutual Improvement Association (YLMIA), she helped write editorials for the *Young Women's Journal* and spoke in public, traveling extensively.[35] Her highest learning during this time, however, probably occurred in the temple, which she attended once a week until her age and health prevented her from going any longer. She wrote in her journal: "I have been working in the temple, and I enjoy this work very much indeed. It is lovely in the temple. I always feel the influence of that sacred place and wish I could go oftener."[36]

Eternal Ties

One incident that revealed both Augusta's and Lucy's spiritual sensitivities involved the latter's youngest child, a son named after his father. Fondly referred to as "Hebey" by his sisters and associates, he had a hip disease, which required that he walk with crutches. Although his father had great hopes that he would "live to spread the gospel at home and abroad," at age seven he became very ill and was soon on his deathbed. Just an hour before Hebey died, Heber, ever close to the spirit, had a strange dream. He dreamed that Lucy and a messenger came to take Hebey while Heber was asleep. In his dream Heber fought with the messenger and finally was able to wrench the boy away from him, unwilling to allow him to depart from his mortal existence. Yet during the fight, he accidentally stumbled and fell upon Hebey's sore hip, causing little Hebey even more intense pain. In his dream Heber ran out of the house to escape the terrible screams of his son and met Brother Joseph E. Taylor. When he told him what had occurred, Brother Taylor gave Heber some sound advice. He said in the dream:

> Well, Heber, do you know what I would do if my wife came for one of her children—I would not struggle for that child; I would not oppose her taking that child away.

> If a mother who had been faithful had passed beyond the veil, she would know of the suffering and the anguish her child may have to suffer. She would know whether that child might go through life as a cripple and whether it would be better or wiser for that child to be relieved from the torture of life. And when you stop to think, Brother Grant, that the mother of that boy went down into the shadow of death to give him life, she is the one who ought to have the right to take him or leave him.[37]

Heber agreed with his friend, and was soon awakened from his dream by his brother who told him that his son was in fact dying.

Heber entered the front room and sat down, with an empty chair between Augusta and him. He felt the presence of Lucy sitting in the chair and truly believed she had in fact come to take her son. Without telling Augusta his feeling, he turned to her and asked her if she felt anything strange. "Yes," she replied. "I feel assured that Heber's mother is sitting between us, waiting to take him away." Apparently, the love that had existed between Heber, Lucy, and Augusta on earth continued beyond the veil to such a degree that Augusta was privileged to be a part of this sacred experience. Later Heber reported, "My living wife, my brother, and I, upon that occasion experienced a sweet, peaceful, and heavenly influence in my home, as great as I have ever experienced in my life."[38]

A Mission to Japan

After eight years of being able to live together, Augusta and Heber faced separation again when Heber was called to open the mission in Japan. Although Lorenzo Snow had given him a year to prepare to leave, Elder Grant needed only half that time to get his personal finances in order. After a series of meetings and dinners offering good tidings and farewell to the member of the Twelve, on 24 July 1901 Elder Grant left for Japan with three other missionaries: Alma O. Taylor, Louis A. Kalesh, and Horace S. Ensign. Of this parting, Augusta recorded, "Our Japanese missionaries have gone. I felt as if there had been a funeral in the house after Heber had gone. I never felt so lonely before when he went away, but then he has never been so far nor for so long. My best hope now is that I can soon go to join him, and that was his last wish also."[39] When Heber returned for the next April conference, in 1902, he went back to Japan with Augusta and their daughter, Mary, who was thirteen years old.

The day they departed Salt Lake, 26 June 1902, Lutie, Lucy's second daughter, was married to George J. Cannon. The entire Tabernacle Choir came to the wedding reception, singing to the Grants to send them off on their way to Japan. Augusta wrote, "It sounded like the singing of angels, and the tears rolled down my face as I stood outside on the porch and gazed up at the stars and thought how long it might be before I saw my home again. Soon we went to the Union Pacific station where several hundred people had congregated to see us off."[40]

Augusta and Heber were companions in Japan for just over a year, attempting to preach the gospel to the people there. Many had expected a great harvest in Japan similar to what had occurred in the Hawaiian Islands; the work was difficult, however, and there were few baptisms. The living conditions also posed a challenge, and Augusta tried to make the best of it that she could. She wrote in her journal about the humidity and rain that made everything moldy and made her perspire so much that it dripped off her ears and kept her hair wet all the time. She also noted, "The mosquitoes are very bad. We have to have a heavy, smelly, green netting suspended from the ceiling over each bed."[41] As the mission home was near the edge of a parade ground where soldiers were trained for battle, each morning the family was awoken by the sound of the bugle calls and put to sleep at dusk by the same bugle call, eerily combined with the bells ringing from a nearby church. Sometimes, as a form of entertainment, Augusta and Mary watched the soldiers practice their sham battles in the courtyard.[42]

Augusta was quite good at learning the new language, having studied French for most of her life, but Heber never picked it up very well, but not for lack of trying. His daughter noted, "Try as he would with all of the patience and persistence which had characterized his whole life, it was of no use. As he remarked many times, the people simply couldn't understand their own language when he spoke it."[43]

While Augusta and her daughter stayed busy with events at home, Elder Grant was busy working hard presiding over the mission.

We prayed earnestly every day for the guidance of the Spirit
of God. We fasted and prayed often. We had a delightful
time. Time passed very pleasantly and did not hang upon
our hands. I never spent an hour in sightseeing. . . . I was
busy all the time, talking with those that called upon me,
answering letters, and in studying the language. The Lord
granteth unto men according to their desires, whether it be
for life or death, joy or remorse of conscience; and the only
desire that I had was to fulfill my duty in that land from
day to day, and if I should return after three or five years
without converting or baptizing one soul I would be satisfied. However, I have been exceedingly grateful to my
Heavenly Father that He saw fit to impress with His Spirit a
couple of men who, I believe, are honest.[44]

Time flew by quickly, and soon it was Christmastime, with the
family trying to celebrate just as they would at home. Augusta wrote:

This is such a beautiful, bright day. I am sitting in my
bedroom upstairs with the windows open and the sun
shining in just like a spring day. From my windows I have
a fine view of Fujiyama, the great volcanic mountain that
the people consider to be sacred and that we see pictured
on so many different things. I look out into our garden
and see one tree full of buds just ready to burst into bloom.
There is a whole hedge of camellias. We have a bouquet of
these waxlike flowers which look like big roses on the table
all the time. This whole great city is one large flower
garden. We are making preparations for Christmas just as
nearly like what we have at home as possible.[45]

In the end not many were baptized in Japan, yet there were a few
faithful members there, and some had sought to defend the Church
against the onslaughts and attacks it was facing. Elder Grant came
home a year early because there were so few fruits of his labors in
Japan. He was a little discouraged, but felt he had done his best and
could do no more.

A Mission to Europe

Following his mission to Japan, Emily greatly anticipated Heber being home to spend time with her and the children. However, in the October 1903 general conference it was announced that Heber J. Grant had been called to preside over the European mission. Emily left the conference and went home, unable to bear the thought of another three years of separation from her husband while she had four young children at home. Shortly after the conference, Heber came bounding home filled with excitement about his new calling, only to have Emily throw her arms around his neck and cry on his shoulder. Heber, always fair, had taken Augusta to Japan and now informed Emily that she and her children would accompany him to Europe.[46]

Emily was very excited about this opportunity. Had she been able to choose between the two missions, she surely would have chosen to go to Europe. For many years she had wanted to return to Britain with Heber. For Emily and Heber the European mission afforded them opportunities to get to know one another better, almost like the honeymoon they had never taken.[47] Heber enjoyed her company and enjoyed the opportunities to travel with her. Emily was always ready to see a play or a concert, and she took her daughters to many of these events. They were even able to enjoy lessons in art and music.

Heber and his wife Emily Wells Grant visit Venice, Italy,
at the end of their European mission, ca. 1906.

Heber wanted to share this opportunity with all of his children and invited his other daughters to see him while he was in England. Their arrival always gave him great joy.

Emily particularly enjoyed finally living the life with her husband that she had always dreamed of. She accomplished much good among the British Saints as they were drawn to her for her wit and wisdom, and many loved her and enjoyed her company.[48] However, not long after they returned from Europe, Emily, the mother of four daughters and a son who died when he was four, was diagnosed with stomach cancer. For a second time, Heber found himself documenting in his journal the demise of a cherished wife. On 23 May 1908 he wrote, "Unless there is a change for the better, she cannot live but a few days." His assessment proved to be correct, and Emily died two days later. The funeral took place on 27 May—what would have been their twenty-fourth anniversary. Concerning the timing of these events, Heber commented, "It seems rather strange that I should be attending her funeral on the anniversary of our wedding. I am sure that she would sooner be buried on this day, however, than any other day in the year. From the time we were married, I have never been separated from her on the 27th [of May] . . . without writing her a letter, expressing my appreciation for our love, and my gratitude to the Lord for our union."[49]

With Emily's death, Augusta remained Heber's only living wife. The two lived and traveled together happily into old age, secure in the knowledge that they would meet again all members of their family who had passed on beyond the veil.

NOTES TO CHAPTER 4

1. Heber J. Grant, "Beginning Life Together," *IE*, April 1936, 198.
2. Rachel G. Taylor, "Temple Work Should Be Done," *IE*, November 1941, 657.
3. Grant, "Beginning Life Together," 198.
4. Bryant S. Hinckley, *Heber J. Grant: The Life of a Great Leader* (Salt Lake City: Deseret Book, 1951), 79.
5. Ibid., 80.

6. Ibid., 81–82.
7. Ibid., 82.
8. Mary Grant Judd, "A Mormon Wife: The Life Story of Augusta Winters Grant," *IE,* July 1945, 425.
9. Hinckley, *Heber J. Grant: The Life of a Great Leader,* 89.
10. Judd, "A Mormon Wife," July 1945, 426; emphasis in original.
11. Ibid.
12. Ibid., 84–85.
13. Hinckley, *Heber J. Grant: The Life of a Great Leader,* 90.
14. Judd, "A Mormon Wife: The Life Story of Augusta Winters Grant," *IE,* August 1945, 451; emphasis in original.
15. Judd, "A Mormon Wife: The Life Story of Augusta Winters Grant," *IE,* October 1945, 574; emphasis in original.
16. Ibid.
17. Ibid., 614.
18. Ibid., 575.
19. Lucy Grant Cannon, "My Beloved Children," p. 12, box 1, folder 13, Jean Willis Cannon Collection, L. Tom Perry Special Collections, Harold B. Lee Library, Brigham Young University, Provo, Utah.
20. Lucy Grant Cannon, "A Father Who Is Loved and Honored," *IE,* November 1936, 682.
21. Lucy Grant Cannon, "My Beloved Children," 23.
22. Francis M. Gibbons, *Heber J. Grant: Man of Steel, Prophet of God* (Salt Lake City: Deseret Book, 1979), 80.
23. Lucy Grant Cannon, "My Beloved Children," 23.
24. Gibbons, *Heber J. Grant,* 80.
25. Grant, "In the Hour of Parting," *IE,* June 1940, 330.
26. Judd, "A Mormon Wife: The Life Story of Augusta Winters Grant," *IE,* December 1945, 754.
27. Ibid.
28. "President Grant Relates Incidents to Promote Faith," *Deseret News Church Section,* 21 November 1931, 2.
29. Cannon, "A Father Who Is Loved and Honored," 682.
30. "President Grant Relates Incidents to Promote Faith," 2.
31. Judd, "A Mormon Wife," December 1945, 755.
32. Ibid.
33. Judd, "A Mormon Wife: The Life Story of Augusta Winters Grant," *IE,*

January 1946, 20; emphasis in original.

34. Judd, "A Mormon Wife: The Life Story of Augusta Winters Grant," *IE*, February 1946, 121.

35. Judd, "A Mormon Wife: The Life Story of Augusta Winters Grant," *IE*, March 1946, 152–53.

36. Ibid., 153.

37. Grant, "In the Hour of Parting," 330, 383.

38. Ibid.

39. Judd, "A Mormon Wife: The Life Story of Augusta Winters Grant," *IE*, April 1946, 216.

40. Ibid., 217.

41. Ibid., 229.

42. Ibid., 229–30.

43. Ibid., 230.

44. CR, April 1902, 46.

45. Judd, "A Mormon Wife," April 1946, 230–32.

46. Hinckley, *Heber J. Grant: The Life of a Great Leader,* 91.

47. Ronald W. Walker, "Heber J. Grant's European Mission, 1903–1906," *Journal of Mormon History* 14 (1988): 24.

48. Hinckley, *Heber J. Grant: The Life of a Great Leader,* 93.

49. Gibbons, *Heber J. Grant,* 148–49.

∿ FIVE ∾

FOR THE WELFARE *of the* SAINTS

On one of his numerous trips to Arizona, Heber J. Grant found himself in Phoenix with fellow Church leader Elder John Henry Smith. The state legislature was in session, and several legislators desired to hear the two men preach. They offered to rent the opera house and procure an audience if Elders Grant and Smith would consent to speak. Since, as Elder Grant explained, they were accustomed to hiring out a hall and then preaching to "empty benches," the elders welcomed the chance.[1] During Elder Grant's discourse, a Church member in the audience overheard a blind man comment on the preaching. Elder Grant recalled that the man said, "'Well, that man is a pretty red hot talker, and seems quite earnest.' Pretty soon he exclaimed, 'I'll be damned if that fellow don't talk earnest.' Not many minutes passed, and he said, 'I'll be damned if I don't believe that fellow believes what he is saying.'"[2] Though Heber acknowledged that some may not see the man's observation as a compliment, he considered it of the highest sort.[3]

Elder Grant could speak passionately on subjects he felt were vital to his listeners. And from the beginning of Grant's tenure in the Quorum of the Twelve and continuing on through his Church presidency, there were certainly no two subjects that he spoke about more earnestly than home industry and the Word of Wisdom. These topics were not merely the subjects for speeches; rather they mandated a way of living, a way of approaching the world. And he believed in living what he preached. He explained, "I have heard some of my own acquaintances preach remarkably fine sermons on tithing, and I have taken the opportunity to look up their records, because I knew they were neglecting their duty, and I found there was no credit on the tithing record." Heber went on to emphasize, "The record is what counts."[4] When it came to home industry and the Word of Wisdom there were few with a more impressive record than he.

"Burned into My Very Bones": Supporting Home Industry

Heber's enthusiasm for home industry stemmed in part from the numerous discourses Brigham Young gave on the subject and the recognition that President Young spoke on behalf of the Lord. The need to "become self-sustaining, to build up the industries of this country," as Heber told the Saints, had been "burned into my very bones."[5] This teaching had been one that Brigham Young instituted in the early days of the Mormon settlement in Utah. In 1852, President Young told the Saints that if they "dispense[d] with every article of manufactured goods, except such as were manufactured" by their families or produced within the territory, it was his opinion they would "find their own interest materially advanced, and the circulating medium would soon find its home in the Territory, instead of traveling to Eastern cities."[6] This teaching, however, was not unique to Young and the conditions in Utah. In 1843 Joseph Smith had tried to help the Saints understand this same principle. As the Prophet told them, "There are too many merchants among you. I would like to see more wool and raw materials instead of manufactured goods, and the money be brought here to pay the poor for manufacturing goods . . . instead of going abroad to buy goods."[7] Thus, in advocating that the turn-of-the-century Saints do likewise and keep their money home to benefit the community, Heber was in good standing with his prophetic predecessors.

Because Grant tended to see the world through money-colored glasses, he saw the fiscal sense this teaching made. Echoing Richard Young's statement that Heber's religious devotion "is practical, everyday, common-sense devotion to principles which from their superiority to all others, he chooses to believe are divine,"[8] Heber declared that "from a practical everyday standpoint, I know that it is beneficial to any community to raise and manufacture those things which they use."[9]

So often did he encourage Church members to purchase goods made in the territory that he earned a reputation among the Saints.

Toward the end of a lengthy speech on the subject, Elder Grant acknowledged, "They say I am a crank on home manufacture. Perhaps I am, and I am proud of the appellation, if it means that I am an enthusiast in that direction. I do not believe we accomplish very much in life unless we are enthusiastic, unless we are in earnest, and unless we practice what we preach."[10] It was this ever-practical approach—to practice what he preached—that underscored every speech he gave on this topic; it was from his own experience that he drew most of the examples used. Speeches on home industry almost invariably included mention of the Provo Woolen Mills. With dogged repetition, he told the Saints, "From the time that I was a boy of sixteen, until the factory closed, with only two or three exceptions, I never wore a suit of clothes that was not made of cloth manufactured at Provo." One suit he purchased during a six-month stay in California. Costing twice as much, it was of far inferior quality. Concerning the suit, Heber reported, "I was ashamed of it at the end of four months, and gave it away."[11] A second suit was purchased when as a member of the territorial legislature he had to buy a black suit so as not to "be the only 'white sheep' in the crowd" at a formal ball. Ever conscious of the need to practice what he preached, Heber gave the suit away the very next day "for fear I might want to preach home manufacture when I had it on, and that the chips would fly back in my own face."[12]

In his preaching Heber was quick to acknowledge that his audience did not share his enthusiasm for home industry. At one conference he addressed those gathered: "Before me is an audience of at least five to ten thousand people, and I would like to know how many of you are standing, or sitting I should perhaps say, with your feet in homemade shoes. I dare not ask those of you who are thus shod to stand up—I am afraid the showing would be altogether too thin." Heber, of course, would have been in the minority standing. "I am myself standing in homemade shoes; it is the kind I have been standing in for over thirty years, and I find that they are good enough for me."[13] As Apostle and prophet during recessions and depressions, he was intimately concerned for the financial welfare of the Church and its members. He also was not hesitant to chide those who disregarded this counsel. "We know that we can and ought to purchase those things that are manufactured here at home," he said, "and but for the selfishness and the narrow-mindedness of the people, we would not have to be called upon to patronize these institutions. If we loved Zion, if we loved the building up of the kingdom of God upon the earth, we would do these things of our own free will and accord, and if we would do it, we would benefit ourselves. It is simply short-sighted policy that causes us to fail to do these things."[14]

As a preacher of home industry, Heber spent much of his time encouraging the Saints to see beyond their immediate temporal situations. "Now, if we had wisdom enough to look ahead of our noses—of course, mine is so long I can't look ahead of it. (Laughter.) But, if the people would only stop and take time to think of the ultimate benefits of sustaining home institutions, they would do it." While acknowledging that "the tenderest part of the human anatomy is a man's pocket," he repudiated the notion that a man who "buys shoddy goods" is actually "benefiting himself and saving money."[15] Heber often resorted in his speeches to giving rudimentary economic lessons. "A dollar is just the same as a drop of blood so far as the finances of the country are concerned," he would tell the Saints. "Money is just like the blood that goes through the body over and over again." To illustrate this principle, Heber recounted a story which by 1895 he had already "told [. . .] over and over again,"[16] and it was an account that many an audience heard in the ensuing fifty years. To those in attendance at the October 1909 conference he explained:

> I have preached many times and quoted Bishop Farrell on this subject. He remarked, here in the Assembly Hall, that one of the reasons he bought homemade goods was to keep the money in the country so he would have a chance to get hold of it again. . . . Brother Farrell said he had been coming to conferences here, twice a year, for the past twenty years, and that during all this time, when he paid for his railroad ticket, he had endeavored to do so with a gold piece which he marked, as he knew the railroads were owned by eastern capitalists, and he wondered if he would ever see any of this money again, and he never did. "But,"

he says, "I have marked many and many a five-dollar bill or gold piece that I have paid out for homemade goods, and I have got them back again, time and time again, because the money stayed in the community. Now, to give you a practical illustration," he said, "as I was leaving, on this identical trip, there was a crowd at the Smithfield depot. I saw a man who had made some shoes for my children, and I gave him five dollars in payment of those homemade shoes. He saw a man to whom he owed five dollars, and he gave him the money. This man saw somebody he was owing, and he handed him the money. This man saw another man to whom he was owing five dollars, and he gave it to him. So the five dollars went from one to another until it came to the fourth man, and he gave it back to me, saying, 'I owe you six dollars, and here are five dollars on account.' That five dollar bill cancelled twenty-five dollars of debts just as quick as it takes to tell it, and I put my 'homemade shoes,' figuratively speaking, back in my own pocket."[17]

For Heber, the wisdom was obvious. Yet in refusing to heed prophetic counsel the "Latter-day Saints," he believed, "are sending out the financial lifeblood of this people when we have the power and the ability to keep it at home."[18]

Not only was Heber J. Grant an avid preacher of home industry, he proved to be an effective promoter of goods made in the territory. An expert penman, he sought out the finest materials with which to work, and it was his assessment that the best ink was made locally by George Goddard. To his dismay Heber found that he could not buy the ink anywhere in Salt Lake. "They didn't have it," he reported. "They said it would not sell; that it was not as good ink as some other." As a result he had to purchase the ink from Goddard directly, who had a "cellar full of it." Heber's solution was to create a demand for the home product. During his tenure as instructor of penmanship at the University of Deseret, Heber made it a point to tell every student, "This is the best ink, you can write the best with it, and if you want to learn to write well, you must have good ink. Now, you go to all the merchants and ask for Goddard's ink."[19] The merchants quickly overcame their reluctance, and the shelves soon were stocked with the sought-for ink.

Heber's support for home industry extended far beyond purchasing homemade shoes and suits and promoting Goddard's ink. He put his money where his mouth was and founded numerous home industries. In so doing, however, he not only experienced the Saints' reticence to support these industries as a spiritual leader, but at times he felt it in his pocketbook. He became so involved with such businesses that toward the end of his life, a prominent community member noted that "Heber J. Grant has probably been instrumental in establishing and furthering the cause of more successful inter-mountain industries and institutions than any man living today."[20]

For his first home industry venture he invested the money made from his insurance sales in a vinegar factory. He quickly discovered, however, that "the people and the merchants would not patronize it." When efforts to promote his product proved futile, Heber had a chemist analyze the competing brand, and he discovered the imported vinegar was made with acetic acid. With this knowledge he set out to convince merchants to buy from the Ogden Vinegar Works, but since the imported goods sold "well," he "could not get the patronage." Exasperated, Heber offered to sell one store owner a barrel two-thirds full of vinegar to which the merchant could then add water and his own "mineral poison." The owner refused on the grounds that "he thought that would be wrong; but he went on selling the stuff manufactured that way."[21]

The Grant Soap Factory, which manufactured laundry soap, suffered a similar fate. Although the family "wrote hundreds of letters and enclosed folded circulars telling about the merits of this fine soap," the purchasers were few.[22] As Heber lamented, "The only people who patronized the soap I made were the Chinamen; . . . they bought it almost exclusively; they discovered it was the best they could get in the city. There were, also, a few of the good sisters who patronized it."[23] Heber could not long afford to manufacture a product for which he had so few customers, and production soon ceased. In light of these efforts, Heber believed that "I have a bigger experience account than all the money I am worth; and I have got a lot of this sad experience in trying to build up and establish home institutions and home manufacture."[24]

There were, however, many home business enterprises that contributed not only to Heber's "experience account" but added handsomely to his bank account. In 1884 he joined with his brother Joshua Grant and George Odell to purchase a wagon and farming machinery business. Grant, Odell, and Company became the Cooperative Wagon and Machine Company the following year. "During its first seven years, the company became the largest wagon and implement dealer in Utah, accumulated $100,000 in reserves, and consistently paid an annual return of 12 percent dividend."[25] What started out for Grant and his partners as a $20,000 venture soon became a $2,500,000 company.[26] In 1886 Heber organized the Grant Brothers Livery and Transfer Company after discovering that the livery business was entirely controlled by non-Mormons. Though the company faced stiff competition from existing companies, by 1890 "Grant Brothers Livery was undisputed master of the terrain."[27] Other home institutions founded by Heber included the Home Fire Insurance Company in 1886 and in 1889 the Home Life Insurance Company, both of which aimed to keep premiums from being sent east. Some years earlier Henry Hyde, founder of the Equitable Life Insurance Company based in the East, heard Heber preach and immediately offered to double his monthly salary if he would work only twenty-four hours a week selling insurance for him. Heber refused, however, as he recognized the actual costs to the people.[28]

Heber J. Grant served as a General Authority from 1882–1945.

An Advocate of the Word of Wisdom

Heber's earnestness for living and preaching the Word of Wisdom was unquestionable, and by April 1894 he had become dismayed with the Saints' lack of compliance with the law of health. His frustration, particularly with priesthood leaders in the stakes he visited, had reached its peak. He told those gathered for the April 1894 conference:

> I have become so discouraged, so disheartened, so humiliated in my feelings, after preaching year after year both by precept and example, to realize that there are Bishops, Bishops' Counselors, Presidents of Stakes, and Patriarchs among the Church of God whose hearts I have not been able to touch, that I had about made up my mind that I would never again say Word of Wisdom to the Latter-day Saints. I felt that it was like pouring water on a duck's back. It had seemed to me as if I could not get sufficient of the Spirit of God to penetrate the hearts of the Latter-day Saints.[29]

He had decided, however, to continue preaching on the subject, since during the conference he felt that the Lord approved of his efforts despite the Saints' lack of obedience.

In addressing the Word of Wisdom at this conference, President Joseph F. Smith had asked Elder Grant to discuss not the spiritual blessings of following this law but the temporal. In this regard, who better in the Quorum of the Twelve but Heber to discuss this principle in financial terms? Just as he had an everyday, practical belief in home industry, he sought to convince the Saints of their economic folly in ignoring the Lord's command. Pointing out that the Saints raised approximately five million bushels of wheat a year, Heber then noted that it would take half of that amount "to pay for all that we consume in breaking the Word of Wisdom."[30] Elder Grant wanted to know who amongst them would ever dare light a match to all that wheat, but that was precisely what they did on a yearly basis. He went on to point out what might have been had the Saints saved all they spent on tobacco, alcohol, and coffee in the previous twenty years. According to his estimate, they would have "from thirty-five to forty millions of dollars, or enough to build Salt Lake City."[31] Try as he could, Heber wanted to convince the Saints that living the Word of Wisdom made good business sense—it was truly for their temporal welfare.

Though Elder Grant had approached the topic fiscally per President Smith's request, it became a way of speaking about the subject that he repeated often. Always concerned with the need for the Saints to keep their money at home, he belabored the point in a 1908 conference address: "All the money that has been spent for the breaking of the Word of Wisdom, during the sixty years that we have been in this country,—almost every single, solitary dollar of it, might have been retained in this community, it might have been here accumulating and multiplying, and growing all the time."[32] Then when he later spoke at the YMMIA conference in June of that year, he told those gathered that had the Saints saved the money spent on breaking the Word of Wisdom, they would be the "the wealthiest state west of the Mississippi River."[33] The Saints were smoking, chewing, and drinking away their opportunities for temporal success.

The topic received no less attention after he became President of the Church in 1918. In fact, the financial difficulties faced by the Saints in the early 1920s and during the 1930s provided an excellent backdrop to discuss the financial benefits of this law. The troubles of the Great Depression could largely be avoided, Heber believed, if people had kept the Word of Wisdom. "I have been thinking very seriously of the wonderful condition that the world is in today during the great depression all over the globe, and I am convinced in my own mind, without shadow of a doubt, that a revelation, covering only one page, given by the Lord, the Creator of heaven and earth, to the Prophet Joseph Smith, would solve the problems of the world if it were obeyed by the inhabitants of the earth, not only solve the problems in our own country but in every country."[34] Despite emphasizing the temporal aspects of salvation inherent in the Lord's law of health, Heber did also recognize that it *was* the Lord's law, and as such had deep-rooted spiritual implications. He always held that the word of God took precedence over any temporal reason to obey the law.

Saved by the Word of Wisdom

In part, Heber's enthusiasm for this topic came from personal experience, and he often testified about how living the Word of

Wisdom had benefited his life. "I believe as firmly as I believe that I am standing here before you today that, on three separate and distinct occasions in my life I would have lost my life had I not been an observer of the Word of Wisdom."[35] One of these instances came in 1897 when Heber underwent surgery to remove his appendix. During the operation, the surgeons discovered that he was in the last stages of blood poisoning. Eight of the nine doctors present were certain of his demise. The chief surgeon even told President Joseph F. Smith, "Mr. Smith, you do not need to discuss the possibility or probability of that man's recovery; he cannot live. Why, if he were to live, it would be a miracle, and this is not the day of miracles."[36] Following the procedure, his personal physician, as Heber recalled, "[told me] to send for my shorthand clerk and make my last statement for I could not live."[37] Die, though, he did not.

Grant always credited his remarkable recovery to his adherence to the Word of Wisdom. When apprised by a nurse of the surgeons' prediction, Heber wanted to meet only with the doctor who didn't anticipate his death. When asked the reason for his opinion, the doctor responded, "I have felt the pulse of hundreds and thousands of gentlemen under operations, . . . but I never felt a pulse just like yours. . . . Your heart never missed one single beat of one hour and three quarters . . . while you were under the knife, . . . and I said, that heart will pull him through." Taking the doctor's statement as fact, Heber credited the strength of his heart to following the Lord's counsel. For him his recovery was no miracle, only a "fulfilling of the law."[38]

Campaigning for Prohibition

Although the Church did not take an official stand on the issue, Heber was actively involved in the prohibition movement in Utah from its inception in 1908. Although other members of the Quorum of the Twelve disagreed with his political stance, and some Church leaders thought he was overzealous, Elder Grant made it a religious issue.[39] As the Church already had a spiritual law of prohibition in place, Church members, he believed, ought to naturally lead out in this movement. And Heber did just that.

So involved was Heber in this campaign that Orson F. Whitney believed that "if ever Utah 'goes dry' it will be largely owing to the indomitable will and energetic efforts put forth by this oft-defeated but never discouraged champion of prohibition."[40] When a prohibition bill went before the state legislature in 1909 and then again in 1915, Heber actively lobbied for its passage. Both times the bill was vetoed by the governor, and some suggested the failure in 1909 was due to Heber's meddling in political affairs.[41] Heber also addressed the issue in conference talks, telling the Saints in 1914, "If the whole of Utah should go 'dry!' it would be the one great thing above all others, to my mind, which would be beneficial to this fair state of ours."[42] In 1916 a slogan of the YMMIA became "We Stand for State- and Nation-wide Prohibition," and it was Elder Grant who introduced the motto at the June conference. Active in the nationwide movement, he reported at the 1914 conference of his travels to Columbus, Ohio, for national meetings of the various temperance groups. Then in 1916, he became president of the Utah Federation of Prohibition and Betterment Leagues, a position which prompted him to study the issue further and to write letters to stake presidents and bishops in Utah seeking their support.[43] As with home industry, Heber clearly did more than just preach the topic; he supported it with his pocketbook, time, and energy.

The passage of prohibition on a national level did not end Heber's discourses on the subject. As a movement began to repeal the constitutional amendment, Heber gave the Saints specific counsel on this matter. While governments may debate the wisdom of such a law, Heber was emphatic that God's laws would not be changed. "The Lord says it is not good, and all the legislatures and all the congresses and all the senators and all the officers in the kingdoms of the world can say otherwise, but that will not change the word of the Creator of heaven and earth."[44] Whereas Heber had previously admonished the Saints to vote for prohibition, in October 1933 he urged them to vote against its repeal. He declared, "Let me promise you right here and now that if you vote for the repeal of the Eighteenth Amendment, there will be a great many more professing Latter-day Saints who will be drunkards than there have been while the Eighteenth Amendment has been in force."[45] Furthermore, he was notably annoyed that he had received an unsigned postcard requesting he not speak about the Word of Wisdom.

I request each and every Latter-day Saint within the sound of my voice to read what I said about the Word of Wisdom just six months ago. Every word that I said I meant, and among other things I said I hoped and prayed that we as a people would not vote for the repeal of the Eighteenth Amendment. Really, I was almost tempted this morning to read my whole sermon over again.[46]

When Utah voted in favor of repeal—the deciding vote on a national level—Heber didn't hesitate to express his dismay: "I have never felt so humiliated in my life over anything as that the state of Utah voted for the repeal of prohibition. I do not want to interfere with any man's rights or privileges. I do not want to dictate to any man. But, when the Lord gives a revelation and tells me what is for my financial benefit and the financial benefit of this people . . . I do think that at least the Latter-day Saints should listen to what the Lord has said."[47] And in following years, he continually reminded the Saints of their decision. He was adamant that they had bought into the lies told about prohibition—"No greater lies were ever published," he declared—and they would reap the rewards accordingly.[48]

When it came to speaking of home industry and the Word of Wisdom and living accordingly, no one could suggest that Heber J. Grant was anything but earnest. Never one afraid of repetition, he talked so frequently on these subjects that people were known to comment before coming to conference that they hoped President Grant would find something else to discuss. To this criticism he responded, "I want to say a little about a subject that so many Latter-day Saints say they are sick and tired of. Why are they sick and tired of it? Because they are not doing their duty. No mortal man who is living the Word of Wisdom is ever sick and tired of hearing it preached."[49] Certainly Heber never tired of the subjects, only the Saints' failure to heed his counsel.

NOTES TO CHAPTER 5

1. CR, October 1922, 13.
2. CR, April 1901, 33.
3. CR, October 1922, 13.
4. Heber J. Grant, "As Other Men Judge Us," *IE,* June 1938, 327.
5. *Collected Discourses,* 5:60.
6. *Deseret News,* 25 December 1852; quoted in Leonard J. Arrington, *Great Basin Kingdom: An Economic History of the Latter-day Saints, 1830–1900* (Lincoln: University of Nebraska Press, 1966), 113.
7. *HC,* 6:58.
8. Richard W. Young Diary, November 1882, 2:3–4, Western Americana, Marriott Library, University of Utah, Salt Lake City; quoted in Ronald W. Walker, "Young Heber J. Grant's Years of Passage," *BYU Studies* 24 (spring 1984): 149.
9. CR, October 1909, 26.
10. CR, April 1910, 40.
11. Ibid., 37.
12. Ibid., 38.
13. CR, October 1921, 10.
14. *Collected Discourses,* 5:60–61.
15. CR, October 1909, 27.
16. *Collected Discourses,* 5:61.
17. CR, October 1909, 27.
18. *Collected Discourses,* 5:61.
19. CR, April 1910, 40.
20. Heber M. Wells, "President Grant—The Business Man," *IE,* November 1936, 689.
21. CR, April 1910, 39.
22. Wells, "President Grant—The Business Man," 688.
23. CR, April 1910, 39–40.
24. Ibid., 40.
25. Ronald W. Walker, "Young Heber J. Grant: Entrepreneur Extraordinary," in *The Twentieth Century American West: Contributions to an Understanding,* ed. Thomas Alexander and John F. Bluth (Provo, Utah: Charles Redd Center for Western Studies, 1983), 105–106.
26. CR, October 1934, 126.

27. Walker, "Young Heber J. Grant: Entrepreneur Extraordinary," 112.

28. Bryant S. Hinckley, *Heber J. Grant: Highlights in the Life of a Great Leader* (Salt Lake City: Deseret Book, 1951), 68.

29. *Collected Discourses,* 4:169–70.

30. Ibid., 171.

31. Ibid., 172.

32. CR, April 1908, 27.

33. Grant, "Temperance—Inspirations to Progress," *IE,* August 1908, 784.

34. CR, April 1933, 6.

35. CR, October 1937, 15.

36. Grant, "On the Use of Tobacco," *IE,* September 1922, 960.

37. Ibid., 959.

38. Ibid., 959.

39. Loman Franklin Aydelotte, "The Political Thought and Activity of Heber J. Grant, Seventh President of The Church of Jesus Christ of Latter-day Saints" (master's thesis, Brigham Young University, 1965), 38.

40. Noble Warrum, ed., *Utah since Statehood: Historical and Biographical,* vol. 2 (Chicago and Salt Lake City: S. J. Clarke Publishing, 1919), 15.

41. Aydelotte, "The Political Thought and Activity of Heber J. Grant," 43.

42. CR, April 1914, 25.

43. Aydelotte, "The Political Thought and Activity of Heber J. Grant," 49.

44. CR, April 1933, 7.

45. CR, October 1933, 6.

46. Ibid.

47. CR, October 1934, 129.

48. CR, October 1937, 14.

49. Ibid., 13.

~ SIX ~

As a prominent citizen in Salt Lake City and a leading churchman, Heber J. Grant often plied his business skills on behalf of the Church and its interests. One of the first chances to exhibit his financial prowess came to him two and a half years after his call as a member of the Quorum of the Twelve. From its inception in 1870, the Salt Lake *Herald* had served as an effective opposition to the anti-Mormon press in the valley, as it could respond to opponents in ways the Church-owned *Deseret News* could not.[1] However, by 1885 the paper had become financially untenable, and it needed additional investment funds to continue printing. Fund-raising efforts came up short despite an announcement from President John Taylor requesting the Saints' support for the paper. With $16,000 still needing to be raised, Heber decided that "I would either go under with the *Herald* or save it."[2] He put at risk both his personal finances and those of his wagon company as he mortgaged his home for $2,000 and the wagon company contributed $3,000. He was also soon able to convince reluctant Church members to likewise contribute. For his efforts Heber became the newspaper's majority stockholder.

Though the paper continued to be published, there was no guarantee that Heber would see a return on his investment. The precarious position of his finances, as would happen numerous times, took a toll on his health. He noted in his journal that "I had intended to go to North Jordan to preach [today] but did not consider it wisdom to do so, on account of my extreme nervous condition."[3] Though he had no newspaper experience previously, he quickly became involved in the paper's daily operation. As vice president and then as president he made significant changes by bringing in a new editor and business manager, altering the paper's format, and increasing coverage. He even took up the pen as part of his duties and wrote numerous editorials. With new advertising accounts and subscriptions, "the *Herald* became a great success inside of three years, making $12,000 a year."[4] It was the only time during the newspaper's "checkered career," according to Horace G. Whitney, the paper's new editor under Heber, that "it was in the dividend-paying class."[5]

Raising Money in the East

Not only were the late 1880s very profitable for Heber, but the territory in general benefited from a period of economic prosperity. As the new decade began, thirty-three-year-old Heber joined with his good friend Heber Wells, who had just been voted out of public office, and they decided they "would go out and try to raise the money to start a bank with a capital of $250,000."[6] Heber proved so adept at raising money that he and Wells had $500,000 capital for what came to be called the State Bank of Utah. As the bank was to be yet another successful home industry, Heber did not keep any promotion fees for his contribution. Unfortunately, the bank was established in the spring 1890 at a time which proved to be the end of a great economic boom. Within months the bank found itself in financial peril; it lost half of its deposits and seemed destined to close. Although not owned by the Church, the bank and its finances had quickly become interrelated with those of Zion's Savings Bank and Trust. Thus the bank's financial situation was of critical interest to the Church and its leadership.[7]

As would prove the case over and over, it was Heber's business sense—his ability to accurately assess situations and his determination to prevail despite overwhelming odds—combined with his reliance on the Lord that provided temporal salvation for the Church and its members. "To look at things naturally," Heber reported, "it [the bank] would fail." Despite the ominous signs, Heber received a double assurance that "I could raise the money necessary to save the bank." The first impression came from his prayers. Then President Wilford Woodruff, aware and concerned about the situation, gave

Heber "a most wonderful blessing," which promised that an intended trip to the East would net Heber "all the money that I went after, and more if needed."[8]

Elder Grant's first stop in Omaha made it clear that divine assurances did not mean obtaining the requisite loans would be easy. To raise the necessary cash, he sought to sell loans the State Bank had made to Zion's Cooperative Mercantile Institution. In response to his request that the bank president purchase a note of $12,000 signed by ZCMI, Heber received no money, only advice. The president suggested he go home and, in the light of the difficult times, loan "a little more money than is considered safe and sound, and it will circulate around and come back into your bank and you will be safe." The answer prompted a stern reply from Heber: "Mr. President, I have not come to you for advice, I have come East for money, and if you will not buy one of these notes for $12,000 of Zion's Cooperative Mercantile Institution I will go farther East and get the money."[9]

This initial rejection only furthered his resolve at his next stop in Chicago where he sought a loan of $24,000. The bank president, who dealt with Heber from behind the bank's counter, laughed at the request to purchase the ZCMI notes.

"Mr. Grant," he asked, "how old is your bank?"
"Not quite a year yet."
"How long have you been in the banking business?"
"This is the first time I have been connected with a bank of this kind."

Seeking to help the novice, the bank president offered the same advice given in Omaha. As Heber had done previously, he rejected the counsel and suggested to the man he would stop off in Chicago on the way home and tell him where he got the money. Although money was currently lending at 0.5 percent a day (182.5 percent a year), Heber insisted that he would only pay "six percent, the regular rate to customers." To this ridiculous suggestion, the president replied, "Well, my dear young man, it will be a long time before you come back. You say you will stop and tell me where you got the money. It will be a long while before I see you again." Heber left

Chicago hoping that it would not be as long as the man anticipated.[10]

As he had done at the previous stop, Heber doubled his request and sought a loan for $48,000 from the National Park Bank in New York. Again he was refused, though this time he received no advice—only chastisement. The bank manager said, "The idea of your coming in here almost a stranger and asking for $48,000 [in the midst of a panic]. Why, we would not think of such a thing as giving you the money." Requesting a piece of paper, Heber wrote out his signature and asked the man if he recognized it. "Of course I do," was his answer. "Well, I did not come in here as a gold brick man, I came here as your customer from whom you solicited a bank account. I did not come here to be insulted." Heber went on: "Well, my friend, I am just a young man from the West. I am just thirty-five, and this is my first experience in borrowing money for our bank. I can give you some pointers as to how we do things in the wild and woolly West. When a man tries to borrow money from us and we are not sure of his security, we ask him for some more security, and we talk it over; and if he finally has sufficient security, we let him have the money."[11] Still hoping to deter Heber, the manager quickly pointed out that it was against the bank's policy to let customers meet with their loan committee. The only loan requests considered were those made in writing.

The manager must have thought he finally thwarted Heber. The loan committee was to meet in only a few minutes, and Heber clearly had no time to draft a formal application. Improvising, Heber asked for another sheet of paper and wrote out his request:

> I am asking you to purchase four notes of Zion's Cooperative Mercantile Institution. Being one of the directors of the institution I know it is able to pay these notes as they fall due, and I am giving you these notes with the endorsement of the directors. We bought them without any endorsement. The directors were perfectly willing to put their names on the back of these notes because they know that they will be paid. Now if you do not wish to take the notes of an institution that is as old if not older than your bank, that has never yet failed to meet its obliga-

tions, that now offers you its note with the endorsement of a half-million dollar bank, the endorsement of the directors . . . you take my advice and quit doing business so far away from home.

A worried Heber waited in the bank's offices for the loan committee's answer. "I remained until after the meeting and spent my time praying to the Lord to soften their hearts so that they would give me the money." In direct contrast to the manager's hesitancy, the president was anxious to purchase the notes as he had done so often in the past. In fact, Heber discovered, the previous president had instructed the president "never to fail to buy every Zion's Cooperative Mercantile Institution note that was offered."[12]

Heber got his $48,000 and continued on to other institutions. In forty-eight hours he secured $88,000 in loans. It came to Heber's mind to once again petition the Chicago bank president. Explaining where he obtained the money, all at 6 percent, the telegram contained a bold request: "Kindly wire and ask for their confirmation of having made these loans to me at six percent, and when you get the answers I hope you will wire that I can send you the other $12,000 note for which I need the money."[13] Having already decided to change his Chicago bank account on the return trip through Illinois, Heber was surprised when the president requested that he send the note.

During the next month, Heber secured loans for an additional $226,000 and obtained assurances for more if needed. As promised, Heber stopped in Chicago and reported his additional success. The previous curt, over-the-counter conversation was replaced by a friendly invitation to meet in the president's office where Heber received the agreed-upon money. At the Omaha National Bank, Heber again related his success. So impressed was the bank president that he telephoned the president of the Union Pacific Railroad and told him, "I want you to meet a young man who has borrowed $336,000 in New York during the panic and got it at six percent. The Union Pacific Railroad ought to get acquainted with this young man, he is the kind of man the Union Pacific are dealing with." Heber had succeeded when few thought he could. Even close friends in Salt Lake had scoffed at his attempt.[14]

Financing the Sugar Beet Industry

Upon Elder Grant's return to Salt Lake, President Woodruff quickly reenlisted his expertise to address a pressing financial concern of the Church. Previously, in the spring of 1889, the First Presidency and Twelve had sent out a circular seeking investment monies to construct a sugar factory.[15] Originally John Taylor had thought to set up the sugar industry in Utah. In 1852, he returned from his mission to France, Taylor imported the needed machinery. Without the proper know-how, the plant produced molasses, never sugar. Nearly forty years later, and after some preliminary experiments, Wilford Woodruff was convinced the Saints ought to try again. He commissioned the directors of two leading Church institutions to assess the feasibility of starting anew the sugar industry in Utah. When the report was issued, no one was in favor of the venture. Woodruff was not deterred and called for another study. Although Heber had been on the first committee, and was decidedly against the proposal, President Woodruff still sought his participation. The second report contained the same assessment as the first, to which President Woodruff responded, "Never mind the report. The inspiration to me is to establish the sugar industry."[16]

Despite his professional opinion on the matter, Elder Grant had been "called upon a mission" and was "sent out to ask men to subscribe for stock in the Utah Sugar Company."[17] The sugar factory, however, was a tough sell. Past failures produced reluctance, and many doubted the wisdom of Church leaders meddling in financial matters. To David Eccles, one of the wealthiest Church members and a most astute businessman, Heber took the First Presidency letter requesting that he invest $5,000 or $7,500. Eccles clearly evidenced the doubt harbored by the territory's leading businessmen. He indicated that he "would like to get off at the lowest figure," and then added, "I hope they will buy lumber from me, so I may make a profit on a part of the five thousand dollars; and after I get the stock, if you can find someone who would like to buy it for twenty-five hundred dollars, I will be much obliged to you if you will come and get the stock."[18] Heber later lamented the Saints' reluctance to support the project:

Men who would invest ten, twenty, thirty, fifty thousand dollars in sheep, and then go in debt in addition, would not put more than fifty or sixty dollars in this industry intended to create employment for the Latter-day Saints, and to benefit the farmers. Some rich sheep man, if you showed him a herd of sheep that was worth fifteen thousand dollars, and told him he could have it for fourteen thousand, would . . . borrow the money, and take chances; but he would not borrow money to put into an industry that the man whom God had called to stand at the head of this people desired to have established; he would give the sixty dollars, and say he never expected to see it again, because the business would not succeed.[19]

By fall of 1889, with the money raised, the Utah Sugar Company was founded, and construction began. When the first payment was due in December of the following year, the brethren had only collected $15,000 of the more than $400,000 promised. As previously willing subscribers now faced financial difficulties, the Church had to borrow money to come up with the balance. In addition to Woodruff's inspiration, or perhaps because of it, a driving force behind the plan was the First Presidency's recognition that "there was not a single enterprise of a public character that was calculated to give employment to our people." According to Joseph F. Smith, the First Presidency felt "a responsibility resting upon us which required something be done . . . in the direction of giving employment to our people."[20] Thus, when Heber returned from New York City at the beginning of 1891, Woodruff sent him off again to get the financial backing needed for the new factory.

Seeking additional loans, Heber returned to Chicago and New York, while also making stops in Boston and Philadelphia. On this trip, however, the preeminent Mormon fund-raiser could find no one willing to advance the requisite funds. Trips to San Francisco and other places produced nothing. With no way to completely finance the project, the Church still had a way out of the deal: payment of $50,000 would cancel the contract with the Dyer Construction Company. By this time Heber had his doubts about continuing on with the factory. Along with other leading businessmen, Heber recommended that President Woodruff pay the forfeit fee. The prophet again refused their advice. "Every time I think of abandoning it," Woodruff told the men, "there is darkness; and every time I think of building it, there is light. We will build the factory if it bursts the Church."[21] As such, Heber was not yet done with this mission.

For the last $100,000 Heber sought out his former employer, Henry Wadsworth, the manager of Wells Fargo in San Francisco. Wadsworth had once thought so highly of him that he gave Heber a hundred-dollar bonus, and now the Apostle pleaded with him "that as he believed in me as a boy, to believe in me now as a man and as one of the leaders of the 'Mormon' Church."[22] Old allegiances, however, were not enough to override the financial panic, particularly when prospects for the industry were not good. "He told me it would be impossible to lend the money, that his committee would not make a loan a thousand miles away, on local security, in the midst of a panic."[23] Never one to take an initial rejection seriously, Heber made a proposition: the bank would loan him the money if he could get twenty of the twenty-five leading financial men in the Church to guarantee payment. "Why, Heber," Wadsworth replied, "that is an impossibility, no set of men on the face of the earth would guarantee four Church notes for $25,000 each."[24] At the very least, Heber wanted the opportunity to try. Wadsworth agreed, and he had the Wells Fargo agent in Salt Lake draw up a list containing thirty names. What Wadsworth believed to be an impossibility, Heber quickly accomplished. "I secured twenty-four signatures. Three of the thirty were out of town; one person whose name was on the list I felt sure would decline, so I did not ask for his signature."[25]

Despite his initial misgivings about the factory, Heber was later of the opinion that "the founding of the sugar industry was one of the grandest happenings that could come to the West."[26] Even before the turn of the century, the economic benefits to farmers and the community at large proved President Woodruff's inspiration superior to the financial advice given by the leading businessmen.

Seven Lean Years

The crisis of 1891 was followed by even greater financial difficulties with the depression of 1893. With Church finances in dire straits, the leadership once again turned to Elder Grant.[27] And again he headed to New York, this time in hopes of renewing over $300,000 in loans. One Church leader reported, "This is the most difficult mission Brother Heber has ever undertaken now that financial affairs are tumbling in all directions."[28] Another blessing, this time at the hand of George Q. Cannon, promised Grant he would be successful. Despite finding the market even worse than in 1891, Heber enjoyed some initial success in New York as he renewed about half the loans.

By the beginning of June, Elder Grant faced another problem. Heber Wells, cashier of the State Bank, reported a run on the bank with cash reserves having dropped to only 22 percent of the total deposits, the legal minimum. The financial agreement between the State Bank and Zion's Savings Bank placed them in a position where several large withdrawals from either would close both financial institutions. Also in jeopardy was the firm Heber J. Grant had formed with George Q. Cannon and other leading churchmen, which had secured loans with bank securities.[29] At stake were the personal reputations of Church leaders as well as the Church's ability to procure future loans. What money Elder Grant was able to obtain did not meet the needs in Salt Lake, and Heber Wells wrote on Saturday, 1 July, "Before you receive this it is possible—nay probable you will hear of our suspension."[30]

In part it was Grant's telegram from New York that convinced the bank's board members to remain open, and for a short time in July the worst appeared over. Wells was pleased to write Heber informing that reserves had gone up somewhat, and they had secured additional funding.[31] The good fortune, however, was short-lived, and again the prospects for closing seemed certain. In August Heber noted: "I feel to thank the Lord with all the power of expression that I am capable of that I have been able to stand the pressure of the past month. . . . I think that I should have broken down with the mental strain which has been upon me had it not been that I had more or less education in being anxious during the months of May, June and July."[32] Concerning this time, Heber's wife Augusta recalled: "We lived on cipher dispatches, I used to say. They would come in the early morning, at twelve o'clock at night, at almost any unseasonable hour.

Heber would take the telegram, and I would get out the code, and we would decipher it word by word. It was usually blue as indigo, a wail from the bank or other places, . . . and Heber would sigh . . . and look so troubled that my heart ached to help him."³³

Immediate relief would only come with the needed funds. On 1 September Heber was relieved by finally securing a $100,000 loan, but he became dismayed when the banker delayed payment until the following Wednesday, two days too late to provide the bank's relief.³⁴ On Saturday, 2 September, Heber woke late after only getting a couple hours of sleep. Kneeling down to pray, Heber asked the Lord if the blessings promising him success on this mission might not yet be fulfilled. "I got up feeling cheerful and with the assurance that I should be blessed in getting the money that was needed and a feeling that it would be the mind and will of the Lord that our banks should close in case I was not able to get the money we needed." Heber left his lodgings and headed downtown, not knowing "where to go or what to do." He entered Blake Brothers and Company and met Mr. John Claflin. "I told him frankly of our condition and that I was willing to make any sacrifice in order to save the banks." Though Heber had petitioned him previously, this time Claflin offered a $400,000 loan on the condition he receive $100,000 as commission. "I finally agreed to take half this amount and to pay half the commission that he asked. I had told the Lord in my prayers this morning that I was willing to make any sacrifice that might be necessary even if it was $50,000 if He would open the way for me to get the money needed."³⁵ While Heber saw God's hand in these proceedings, other members of the Twelve were not of the same opinion, and they questioned Heber's judgment.³⁶ Even President Woodruff was none too pleased at the prospects of paying interest on $250,000 while only receiving $200,000.³⁷

When Elder Grant spoke at general conference in October of that year he chided the Saints for their financial foolishness. He pointed out, "This whole financial panic is a great hoax from first to last, in one sense of the word." The "senseless panic," as he called it, had caused 570 banks to fail. "The people all over the country got scared. At what? At nothing. In the face of good crops of cotton, corn and wheat, and general prosperity in the whole country . . . people got scared, drew their money out of the banks and in many cases hid it."³⁸

Even as he pointed out the Saints' folly, he felt the need to make a confession:

> I want to confess to you that I and many others have done wrong. Why? Because we have been so very anxious to make a dollar that we have run in debt, and now we cannot promptly pay our honest debts. I cannot; for the reason that $10,000 collateral securities which are good, would not raise a thousand dollars. For the first time in my life I have had people come to me and ask me to pay money that I owed them, and I have had to ask for an extension of time. If the Lord will only forgive me this once I will never be caught again. I have been a borrower of money since I was eighteen; but if I can only get paid off what I owe now, I shall be content, I believe, with the blessings of the Lord, whatever they may be, be it much or little.[39]

For the remainder of the decade the Grants would have little, rather than much, on which to live.

A Family Burden

Heber best described the ruin that became his finances when he said that "lightning struck me financially." In four short months he went from being worth $100,000 to finding himself $30,000 in debt.[40] His situation deteriorated even further. And as he often came to say, "I was somewhat more than one hundred thousand dollars worse off than nothing."[41] So desperate did the Grants' finances become that a dear friend, Alex G. Haws, a former boarder at Rachel Grant's home and who later offered Heber a position as a vice president of New York Life Insurance Company, offered to mortgage his home, the only way even he could borrow money, in order to save Heber's "financial life." The telegram read: "Telegraph me upon receipt of this letter; do not write because delays are dangerous, and the money shall come to you by first mail." Concerning the offer, Heber explained, "I could not restrain my tears when I read that letter, to think that God had given me sufficient of His Spirit whereby I had been enabled to so live that a man who was an agnostic . . . had been so impressed with the genuineness of my character and integrity that he was willing to risk his home to save my 'financial life.'"[42]

To get out from the enormous burden of debt, others, including close friends who believed his situation was beyond hope, urged Heber to declare bankruptcy. If the law was designed for anyone, they reasoned, it was for Heber. This action, however, he refused to take. "If I live to be a hundred years old," he said, "I will not do it. I will go on working to pay my debts. If some one knocks me down, I cannot help that, but, if a giant tackles me, I will defend myself. And if, after a hundred years, I have not paid my debts, then I will pray to the Lord to let me live another ten years in the hope of doing so."[43] So concerned with meeting his obligations and paying what he owed, that even when a close friend, for whom Heber provided security on a note, opted for bankruptcy, Heber assumed the $12,700 loan that had a $9,000 security. Eventually, Heber reported, "I made a profit of several thousand more than $3,700 by assuming the debt and carrying the securities for a few years."[44]

Getting out of debt became a family affair. With a food and clothing budget of just seventy-five dollars a month, the family of ten

Heber J. Grant's ten daughters. Front row (left to right): Rachel, Mary, Frances, Emily, Grace, Lucy. Back row (left to right): Anna, Florence, Dessie, Edith.

had to learn to economize in ways they had never previously considered. Milk, when served, was limited to a single glass. Stale bread was not thrown out but "might be steamed and eaten hot, or utilized for bread pudding, or fried till nice and brown and eaten with what [the] children called 'Grant stand-by,' in other words, creamed chipped beef gravy."[45] For Christmas that year the Grant children had to go, for the first time in their lives, without a Christmas tree. Heber's two oldest daughters, Rachel and Lucy, quit school at the Latter-day Saint high school and procured office jobs. Even his wife Augusta learned to type so she could contribute to the family earnings. It was common for Heber to work late into the evening, until midnight or later, just to be able to pay the interest owed on $75,000 of his debts. (Several of those to whom Heber was indebted did not require him to pay interest.)

One evening when Heber returned home at one in the morning, he was greeted by his wife. "Heber," she said, "you do not use tea, coffee, tobacco or liquor, but you are breaking the Word of Wisdom, because of working the way you do, more than if you used tea and coffee; and I am not sure that you are not breaking it more than if you were to use tobacco. It is a crime the way you are abusing yourself—" Her mild chastisement stopped abruptly as she launched into a blessing. As she spoke with the gift of tongues, Heber did not understand the pronouncement. When she was finished, together they knelt down and sought the interpretation: "It was that I should live to cancel every obligation I had; that I should live to have a comfortable, happy home, paid for and free."[46]

Notably the blessing did not promise immediate emancipation from the shackles of debt. Rather, there were to be seven lean years before a respite. Concerning the challenges Heber faced, one daughter wrote: "Although he was always hopeful and optimistic, working, planning night and day so that he might be able to get out of debt, I believe those years of anxiety would have broken him down completely had he not had supreme assurance and courage born of his faith in the Gospel of Christ." Their financial condition even made an impression on the children; this daughter further wrote, "I know in those years a horror of financial obligation was born into the souls of those of us who were old enough to see him under this great strain which made us feel that debt was like a huge dragon into whose ugly mouth the very life-blood of its victims was drawn."[47]

By the turn of the century, Heber's situation had improved minimally as he still owed a significant amount of money. His mother's home was mortgaged for $3,000, and, as he explained, "Everything I had would not pay my indebtedness within $25,000 or $30,000."[48] With the $5,000 that he made yearly, and the money earned by his wife and daughters—Rachel made $65 a month, Lucy $30, and Augusta $30—Heber calculated that it would yet be ten years before he "would be free with the world financially."[49] Deliverance was not to come easy, or at least it appeared so.

A Ram in the Thicket

At the beginning of 1901, Heber joined a meeting of the Twelve and the First Presidency at the Salt Lake Temple. George Q. Cannon announced the decision to open a mission in Japan. "And the moment he said it," related Heber, "it came to me as plain as though a voice spoke, 'You will be called to preside there.'" President Cannon talked on for another twenty-five minutes without announcing who was to head up the mission. The interlude between his impression and President Cannon's announcement gave Elder Grant time to debate the prospects of going. His initial thought was, "I cannot go to Japan, seeing that I will lose a little over $5,000.00 a year income." He also recalled, however, that whereas he recently had been "$100,000 worse than nothing," he "was now only $25,000 or $30,000 worse off than nothing." Recognizing what he clearly saw as divine intervention in his financial affairs he decided, "I will accept the mission, and under no circumstances will I make any excuse whatever."

As Cannon talked on, Elder Grant thought to himself, "Will he never announce that I am to be made president of the Japanese mission?" Finally Cannon said, "We hear that Brother Grant has overcome all his great financial difficulties and has announced that he is going to take a trip around the world to celebrate his financial freedom and we have decided to stop him half way around at Japan, to preside." When President Lorenzo Snow inquired if he had made such a remark, Heber pointed out that Cannon had disregarded an important qualifier: *if.* Wanting to better understand the elder's position, President Snow probed Heber about his finances. Heber's replies were purposefully vague, not wanting to give reason for the prophet to rescind the call. "As Brother Snow was talking the thought came to me: 'It is not an excuse to tell your condition financially,' and I remarked to myself, 'Shut up, Mr. Devil, if I should tell my condition financially there isn't a man in this room that would let me go to Japan. That is the best excuse I could possibly make.'"[50] Heber left the meeting with the call in place, and President Snow had given him a year to make the necessary preparations to take leave of his family and businesses.

Before Elder Grant departed the temple, his fellow Apostle John W. Taylor asked to meet with him. "Heber," Taylor told him, "you have made a financial sacrifice today that is the equal, financially speaking, of Abraham offering up Isaac. The Lord accepted the offering and provided the ram in the thicket to save Isaac. The Lord has accepted your offering. I know your condition financially, and I prophesy that you shall be blessed of the Lord and make enough money to go to Japan a free man financially."[51] Taylor explained that Heber was not "to plan to make any money." Rather he was to kneel each morning in prayer and supplicate the Lord regarding how he could make money that day. Not wanting to wait until the next morning, Heber went home and explained to the Lord he wanted to make some money that very day. An impression came: "Get the Utah Sugar Company to pay a stock dividend, and the value of your stock will increase, and you can sell it for more than the present price, to help you cancel your debts."[52] In heeding the suggestion, Heber quickly made $30,000. At the end of four months Heber had paid $4,600 in tithing. In August 1901, the *Improvement Era* announced Heber's miraculous success: "[Heber] had now to relate that God, in a marvelous way, had blessed and prospered him to that degree that within the past few months he had been enabled to cancel one hundred thousand dollars of his indebtedness, and was, at this moment, practically free from financial embarrassment and distress."[53]

118

8 of the Herald and Heber's purchase of the paper, see

NOTES TO CHAPTER 6

1. For a discussion of the *Herald* and Heber's purchase of the paper, see Ronald W. Walker, "Young Heber J. Grant: Entrepreneur Extraordinary," in *The Twentieth Century American West: Contributions to an Understanding*, ed. Thomas Alexander and John F. Bluth (Provo, Utah: Charles Redd Center for Western Studies, 1983), 107–108.
2. Heber J. Grant to Charles L. Anderson, 8 December 1885, Letterpress Copybook, 6:247–48; quoted in Walker, "Young Heber J. Grant: Entrepreneur Extraordinary," 107.
3. Heber J. Grant Manuscript Diary, 22 November 1885, 7:213; quoted in Walker, "Young Heber J. Grant: Entrepreneur Extraordinary," 108.
4. Heber M. Wells, "President Grant—The Business Man," *IE*, November 1936, 688.
5. Noble Warrum, ed., *Utah since Statehood: Historical and Biographical*, vol. 2 (Chicago and Salt Lake City: S. J. Clarke Publishing, 1919), 13.
6. Ibid.
7. Ronald W. Walker, "Crisis in Zion: Heber J. Grant and the Panic of 1893," *Arizona and the West* 21, no. 3 (fall 1979): 260.
8. CR, April 1942, 4.
9. Ibid., 5.
10. Ibid.
11. Ibid., 5–6.
12. Ibid., 6.
13. Ibid., 7.
14. Ibid., 8.
15. For a discussion of the Utah Sugar Company, see Leonard J. Arrington, *Great Basin Kingdom: An Economic History of the Latter-day Saints, 1830–1900* (Lincoln: University of Nebraska Press, 1966), 386–91.
16. Heber J. Grant, "Inspiration and Integrity of the Prophets," *IE*, August 1919, 845.
17. Ibid.
18. Ibid., 846.
19. CR, October 1903, 9.
20. Quoted in Arrington, *Great Basin Kingdom*, 388.
21. Grant, "Inspiration and Integrity of the Prophets," 846.
22. Grant, "Significant Conference Themes," *IE*, June 1922, 709.

23. Grant, "A Domestic Sugar Supply," *IE,* September 1936, 524.

24. Grant, "Significant Conference Themes," 709.

25. Grant, "A Domestic Sugar Supply," 525.

26. Grant, "Significant Conference Themes," 710.

27. For a discussion of Grant's business activities during 1893, see Walker, "Crisis in Zion," 257–78.

28. Francis Lyman Diary, May 10, 1893; quoted in Walker, "Crisis in Zion," 264.

29. Walker, "Crisis in Zion," 265–66.

30. Quoted in Francis M. Gibbons, *Heber J. Grant: Man of Steel* (Salt Lake City: Deseret Book, 1979), 95.

31. Ibid., 95–96.

32. Ibid., 96.

33. Mary Grant Judd, "A Mormon Wife—The Life Story of Augusta Winters Grant," *IE,* January 1946, 20.

34. Walker, "Crisis in Zion," 275.

35. Quoted in Gibbons, *Heber J. Grant,* 97. See also Walker, "Crisis in Zion," 275.

36. Davis Bitton, *George Q. Cannon: A Biography* (Salt Lake City: Deseret Book, 1999), 345. Cannon felt the cost was too high: "This is a frightful sacrifice—equal to 20 per cent per annum; but brother Grant is willing to make desperate efforts to save the banks. Pay day is coming, however, and what then?"

37. Walker, "Crisis in Zion," 276. Concerning those who second-guessed him, Heber believed they did not "comprehend the exigencies of the case," and he "would gladly have given twice as much had it been necessary in order to save our banks."

38. *Collected Discourses,* 3:373.

39. Ibid., 3:374.

40. Judd, "A Mormon Wife," January 1946, 20.

41. "President Heber J. Grant's Seventieth Anniversary," *IE,* November 1926, 19.

42. CR, April 1901, 32.

43. CR, October 1934, 127.

44. CR, October 1933, 7.

45. Judd, "A Mormon Wife," January 1946, 20.

46. "President Heber J. Grant's Seventieth Anniversary," 19–20.

47. Lucy Grant Cannon, "A Father Who Is Loved and Honored," *IE*, September 1936, 681.

48. Grant, "Ram in the Thicket," *IE*, December 1941, 713.

49. Ibid., 765.

50. Ibid., 713.

51. Ibid.

52. Ibid., 765.

53. "A Farewell Reception," *IE*, August 1901, 797.

~ SEVEN ~

SERVICE *in the* YMMIA

No other man living has so long a record of unbroken service to the young people of this Church as Heber J. Grant.[1]

—Bryant S. Hinckley

On 9 June 1895, one day before the twentieth anniversary of the organization of the Young Men's Mutual Improvement Association (YMMIA), Heber J. Grant addressed the association members who had gathered at the Tabernacle for the annual conference. During the previous twelve years as a member of the Quorum of the Twelve, Elder Grant had been able to dedicate little time to "Mutual Improvement." However, prior to his apostolic call, Heber had been intimately involved with the program: as an officer in the first association organized, then as his ward's president, and then in 1880 as secretary to the general superintendent, Wilford Woodruff. Now fifteen years later, Woodruff was both President of the Church and leader of the YMMIA. He again sought out Heber's help with the program, calling him to be an assistant to the General Superintendency, composed of President Woodruff, Joseph F. Smith, and Moses Thatcher.

As Elder Grant addressed the conference attendees, he explained his abiding interest in this Church program. Since the organization of the first association, he said,

> I have ever taken an interest in the Mutual Improvement Association because of the realization of the fact that as a young man I stood as it were upon the brink of usefulness

or upon the brink of making a failure of my life, and to a
certain extent I give the credit to the Mutual Improvement
Associations and to the Sunday School that I have become
a faithful member in the Church of Christ.

He expressed his gratitude for the men who had provided guidance
for him—among them Hamilton Park and George Goddard—at a
time when his faith had wavered, and "I was tempted seriously for
several years to renounce my faith in the Gospel."[2] It was the association with these men, the opportunity to be a Sunday School teacher
and MIA president, and interaction with the young people his age
that provided Heber with spiritual uplift he needed at that time. Were
it not for these Church programs, Heber readily acknowledged that
he might never have attained his lofty ecclesiastical position. This
1895 call marked his reintroduction to YMMIA, an involvement that
would continue for the next fifty years.

Mutual Improvement in the Valley

The Saints' desire for cultural and scientific refinement began
almost as soon as they arrived in the Salt Lake Valley. A participant in
a group that began meeting in 1849 wrote, "Some of the young
[men] formed themselves into a class for improvement, called mutual
improvement class."[3] In 1852 the "Polysophical Society" was founded
by Lorenzo Snow. Composed of the leading men and women in the
Church, the group's meetings focused on "essays, poems, recitations,
music, song, anecdote, experience and comment," which according to
a former member, "made a veritable 'feast of reason and flow of
soul.'"[4] The society's demise came about during the reformation
period from 1856 to 1857.[5] From that time on, there were numerous
literary societies, debating clubs, and young men's organizations inde-
pendently set up for the betterment of family and friends.

In the growing tradition of mutual improvement, the Wasatch
Literary Association began in February 1874 as Orson Whitney and
friends organized a reading society that would further their intellectual interests as well as their interests in the young women whom they
sought to court. With Whitney as president and Emma Wells as
secretary, the group met each Wednesday for the purpose of "the

social advancement and the improvement of its members in general literature, music, and drama."[6] The members, generally in their late teens and early twenties, were completely responsible for the lectures, debates, and impromptu speaking; the essays, parodies, and poetry read; and the music and dramatic productions performed. As part of what was called the "Budget Box," original compositions from the members were read each week. A critic was selected to provide commentary on the pieces and, as Orson Whitney explained, to "tone down the risibilities of fun-loving members who evinced at times a disposition to sacrifice everything for a laugh."[7]

Acquainted with many association members, Heber first attended meetings as a guest in early 1876, participating in a dialogue performed on 26 April. On 17 May Heber formally joined the "Wasatchers," as they were called, and soon gave two speeches on a topic that he knew well: insurance. As owner of a leading insurance agency in the territory, Heber sought to espouse the virtues of that which provided for his living. The topic, however, was out of step with the highly creative and often humorous productions of other members. The criticism provided during the meetings could often be biting and very personal; Heber recalled shedding "many bitter tears when my grammatical errors and other mistakes were laughed at." While their attacks led him to consider himself "the least beloved and respected of any other members of the Club," he did not desist from the activities.[8] Despite his feelings of being an outsider, Heber continued participating in the verbal sparring that was often part of association meetings and joined members in their social activities.

From the viewpoint of Church leaders and other adults in the community, there were problems with such organizations: they were devoid of supervision and often devoid of religion. There were those who considered the societies to be a little too fun-loving—partaking of a spirit that "seemed too secular, carefree, and at times bruising."[9] While there had been a proliferation of such associations, there were attempts by the Church to influence the movement's direction. By the mid-1870s, for example, at least five of the twenty Salt Lake wards had started similar youth programs. With these organizations clearly responding to the needs and desires of young people, Brigham Young decided that an organization ought to be established separate from the priesthood but guided by it.

The Organization of the YMMIA

On 6 June 1875 Brigham Young sent word to Junius Wells that he wanted the young men to be organized. Providing no additional directions, President Young left that morning with George Q. Cannon for Church meetings in Logan, Utah. Wells met Bishop Woolley of the Thirteenth Ward that Saturday afternoon. The following morning Wells requested that the other Salt Lake bishops announce that a meeting had been planned for Thursday, 10 June, at 7:00 P.M. to proceed with the organization. It was Wells's "expectation that President Young would be present to inaugurate this important movement."[10] On Wednesday, Wells requested the prophet's son, B. Morris Young, to make the rounds amongst the boys and remind them to attend.

An anxious Wells was waiting outside the President's office when Brigham returned from Cache Valley on Thursday morning. Wells related what he had already accomplished, telling him of the meeting scheduled for that evening. He discovered, much to his chagrin, that neither the President nor George Q. Cannon would attend. Brigham Young simply informed Wells what he desired from the organization:

> We want to have our young men enrolled and organized throughout the Church, so that we shall know who and where they are, so that we can put our hands upon them at any time for any service that may be required. We want them to hold meetings where they will stand up and speak—get into the habit of speaking—and of bearing testimony. These meetings are to be for our young men, to be composed of young men for their improvement—for their mutual improvement—a society of young men for mutual improvement. There is your name: The Young Men's Mutual Improvement Soci—Association.

Following Wells's additional inquiries, Brigham explained that the association ought to have officers, including a treasurer and librarian.

The latter was needed as he felt it proper "to collect good books and encourage reading them." At the meetings members were to be called upon to bear their testimonies. As Young explained, "Many may think they haven't any testimony to bear, but get them to stand up and they will find the Lord will give them utterance to many truths they had not thought of before. More people have obtained a testimony while standing up trying to bear it than down on their knees praying for it."[11] The associations were to be not only a place of learning but a place of performance—a place where testimony could be acquired and strengthened through participation.

Wells left this meeting and proceeded to the Thirteenth Ward building, located on Second South. Before the appointed hour the meeting hall was already filled with parents, with Woolley and several other ward bishops seated in the back. The young men, however, had not joined the rest and were milling about outside. When he finally arrived, Wells invited the boys to go in, although, according to B. Morris Young, "some of us hesitated, for we were all bashful." Amongst the group, Young recalled seeing Heber, "for he was the tallest one in the crowd." Upon entering, the boys found places in the audience. As this was to be an organization for the boys run by the

Thirteenth Ward building, where Heber attended church as a young man.

boys under the proper leadership, Wells entreated several of the young men to sit with him on the podium. Though reluctant to do so as they "were too modest to face the people," several finally agreed.[12] Wells's explanation of the program, which took up the bulk of the meeting, reiterated the purposes that he had just learned from President Young. At the meeting's conclusion, eighteen boys signed up. Officers were then announced, including twenty-four-year-old Henry A. Woolley as president and B. Morris Young and Heber J. Grant as counselors, ages twenty-one and eighteen respectively.

Although the organization was founded in June, regular meetings were not held until August. Convening on the nineteenth, the young men in the Thirteenth Ward gathered, as Wells announced, "to inaugurate a series of such meetings among the young people of this city."[13] A secretary, H. H. Goddard, was appointed to join the previously nominated officers, all of whom were once again sustained. As before, Wells spoke of the organization's purposes. The boys, Wells announced, would meet "together in an organized capacity" so that they might be "protected from many temptations and snares of the enemies of our people." They would seek, he went on to say, "the cultivation of the heart as well as of the mind" in developing and strengthening testimonies.[14] Bishop Woolley addressed the boys when they met next on Monday, 23 August, at which time he suggested their objective "was to learn more about the Religion we had embraced, and speak upon the different Principles of the Gospel commencing with Faith." When the meeting was adjourned, the secretary noted in the minutes: "The subject of Faith was selected to speak upon at the next meeting."[15] In accordance with Brigham Young's original instructions, each boy at the 30 August meeting got to speak when his name was called. It was often the case, however, that when the young men would "rise and make a few remarks" they were heard to announce, "I am not prepared to speak on the subject tonight," or they provided the "frequent assurance that 'the gospel we believe in is the restored gospel, proved by the scriptures.'" At other meetings the boys were better prepared. When they discussed the Word of Wisdom the minutes kept that evening noted that "Brother H. J. Grant spoke a few minutes and said, if a person had any sense at all he could see that tobacco and whisky were not good for the human system, as nearly everybody that uses tobacco had to make themselves sick the first time they tried it."[16]

President of the Thirteenth Ward YMMIA

Junius Wells's affiliation with the YMMIA was interrupted when he left on 1 September 1875 to serve a mission in the eastern United States. Prior to his departure Wells had established associations in several Salt Lake wards as well as in Brigham City and a few other towns. To further the YMMIA work, Brigham Young called on his twenty-one-year-old son, Morris, along with Milton H. Hardy, a recently returned missionary from England, and twenty-six-year-old John Henry Smith, a future member of the Twelve. The three men were directed by Brigham to "travel throughout the territory" with the intent to "visit every settlement and organize in each ward these associations."[17] With Morris Young's departure in December to perform the assigned work, new officers were called in the Thirteenth Ward association, with Heber J. Grant becoming the new president.

It was in Heber's position as association president that Bishop Woolley made the enthusiastic young man responsible to raise money for completion of the St. George Temple. Other wards had already held fund-raisers, and Woolley approached Heber about hosting a dance: "Now, I want you to get up a party; you have more friends among the young people than anyone; I want you to choose your own committee and arrange the whole thing and turn over the proceeds to us for the benefit of the St. George Temple." The driven bishop added a direct challenge: "I want you to make a success of it. We generally lead every other ward in everything we try to do. I want you to be sure to beat them all." The chances of putting on a successful dance, however, were handicapped by several of the bishop's own policies. He wouldn't allow, for example, ward members to wax the rough-board floor with candle shavings since he did not want "to have people falling down and breaking their necks."[18]

Recognizing what the Saints would require if they were to attend the Thirteenth Ward party, Heber had to wrest several important concessions from the independent Woolley. Therefore, in accepting this call, Heber told him that he had to "agree to pay the loss if there is one." The response caught the bishop off guard, as he planned to make the largest ward donation with the proceeds. Heber went on: "You cannot have the party in the Thirteenth Ward and make any money; the young people won't come any more. In other places they allow them to have three round dances, and you won't have any. I would rather dance three round dances and throw all the rest away. You have got to have three waltzes."[19] Reluctantly the bishop agreed.

As there were other compromises that Heber sought, he pushed further: "You won't allow Olsen's Quadrille Band; they are the only people who can play the Blue Danube Waltz well; that is one of the things that draws the crowd. When you say Olsen's full band, that means the finest cornetist in Salt Lake will be there to give some cornet solos during the evening." Woolley's objection to the band stemmed from a previous Thirteenth Ward appearance during which the flute player got drunk. His drive to succeed outweighed his principles in this case, and he told Heber, "Take Olsen's Quadrille Band; take your three round dances; wax your floor."[20]

Heber proved to be a most capable organizer and promoter as he chose well-placed and adept aides. His assistant, Edwin Woolley, helped Heber turn a classroom into a "fine drawing room," with "President Young's picture and others there, full-size." A boy from the Young family was placed on the committee to ensure that Brigham's family would attend. Heber also selected Nelson Empey and Hyde Young for the committee, and they each promised to get the "boys in ZCMI" and the "railroad boys" from the Utah Central Railroad likewise to be there. Heber sold tickets in advance, and as people arrived at the dance he sat at the entrance and checked them off on his alphabetized list.[21]

With money to be raised, Heber plied his better-than-proficient skills as a salesman. He approached Captain Hooper, president of ZCMI, and invited him to purchase a ticket. Countering the invitation was Hooper's explanation that "I never go to parties." Heber, however, was not to be deterred by the quick rebuff. He told Hooper, "There are two important things about this party, and this is one of them—it is for the benefit of the St. George Temple; and this is the other—tickets are $1.50." Hooper laughed, gave him the money, and said, "Go sell it to Eldredge." Heber approached Brother Eldredge as suggested, and again he was told, "I do not go to parties any more."

Nonetheless, Heber sold him the ticket, and eventually the ticket was sold five or six times before he found a buyer who actually planned to attend.[22]

Attempts to get Brigham Young to purchase tickets for ten of his sons proved fruitless, as the President replied, "Let the boys pay for their own tickets." Brigham did come on the appointed evening, and when he arrived he asked, "This is for the benefit of the St. George Temple, isn't it?" Then, tossing down ten dollars, he inquired if that would pay for his ticket. Heber assured him that it would, and he later recollected, "I do not know whether or not he expected any change, but he did not get any."[23]

The dance was an enormous success. When the following morning President Young requested a list of all those in attendance, Bishop Woolley was pleased to deliver the list and the eighty dollars raised. As the amount was double what any other ward generated, Heber felt they had "scooped the town."[24]

Beyond the Thirteenth Ward: The YMMIA as Churchwide Program

As Mutual Improvement Associations were created in wards throughout the territory, each worked independent of one another to best determine how to achieve the objectives set out by President Young. Recognizing the deficiency of this arrangement, a meeting was announced for YMMIA participants to be convened on 8 December 1876 in the Council House in Salt Lake. Those in attendance selected Junius Wells, recently returned from his mission, to serve as president of the YMMIA Central Committee, assisted by Milton H. Hardy and Rodney C. Badger as counselors. In an effort to coordinate the program's doings, stake superintendents and counselors were called to oversee the ward programs. By 1878 a systematized curriculum was recommended to ward organizations. "These programs consisted of an outline of Bible, New Testament, Book of Mormon and Church History subjects, which were conveniently divided into periods, and embraced, in connection with the historical narrative, some of the leading principles of the gospel."[25] Wards were also directed to have weekly meetings from October to May each year, and once a month there was to be a joint meeting with the Young Ladies Mutual Improvement Association. Stakes were directed to hold quarterly conferences, and every other week visitors from one ward were directed to attend the meetings of another association. The visitors were "not to occupy all the time in preaching, but to observe the exercises of the meeting, and to speak during the time usually allotted to testimony bearing, as they may be requested by the presidents."[26]

The place of the YMMIA as an important Church auxiliary was affirmed in April 1880 when President John Taylor chose Wilford Woodruff to be the organization's general superintendent, with Elders Joseph F. Smith and Moses Thatcher as his counselors. The previous central committee members were reassigned to be assistants to the new apostolic leadership. John Taylor selected as their secretary twenty-three-year-old Heber J. Grant.

Heber gained added responsibilities in October when he was called as a YMMIA missionary. As "the young people [in the Church] had not been accustomed to study," association leadership had difficulties at times installing the desired programs. To this end, "music, songs, recitations, literary entertainments, intermingled with testimonies and religious references were employed" until the point where the young men "became more thoroughly interested in intellectual pleasures." Thus, "the lighter character of the programs of the earlier societies" were dropped, and the leaders were able to guide "the [boys] on into heavier studies."[27] The YMMIA missionaries were to facilitate these changes by "introducing systematic exercises, encouraging the establishment of libraries and reading rooms, extending the circulation of the *Contributor*" along with "preach[ing], exhort[ing], and labor[ing] with the youth as they may be led by the spirit."[28] Heber's participation in the Churchwide leadership was cut short by his call at the end of October 1880 to be the stake president in Tooele.

Call as a Counselor

After a fifteen-year hiatus from the YMMIA, Heber returned to Churchwide leadership in the program with his call in 1895 to be an assistant to the General Superintendency. Less than two years into this assignment, he had grown disenchanted with the state of the program. The association magazine, the *Contributor,* which Junius Wells had begun in 1879 with John Taylor's blessing, ceased production in 1896 due to a lack of support. Rather than meeting weekly to discuss pertinent issues, the general board convened once every six months or so. As Heber explained, "I felt that the law of progress, the law of growth and advancement, in the Young Men's Mutual Improvement Associations was not being fulfilled."[29]

Elder Grant laid blame at the feet of Moses Thatcher: "There was a disorganization of the general superintendency of the Mutual Improvement Associations because of the failure of one of the men in that superintendency to retain his standing in one of the high positions in the Church."[30] Thatcher's standing as a member of the Twelve had been in question since the early 1890s. Poor health prevented him from meeting in council with the Twelve. An addiction to morphine, which he took for his ulcers, further compounded his problems. However, even when healthy, Thatcher neglected his Church duties, focusing instead on his many business ventures. Disagreements with Church leaders over political matters proved to be the last straw, and when Thatcher refused to meet with his fellow Apostles he was summarily dropped from the quorum. Though subsequently tried for his membership, Thatcher demonstrated sufficient humility to avoid being excommunicated.[31]

It was at this time that Heber prayed to take Thatcher's place. He noted, "Twice in my life I prayed to the Lord to be appointed to a position. The first was when . . . I got down on my knees and I asked the Lord to call me to be one of the superintendency of the Young Men's Mutual Improvement Association."[32] The assignment came the following day. Elder Grant recalled:

> The next day I happened to be in the president's office, upon some business, and while I was there a discussion arose as to who should fill the vacancy in the superintendency of the Young Men's Mutual Improvement Association. President Joseph F. Smith turned to President Woodruff and said: "I believe that inasmuch as I am a member of the presidency of the Church, we need not only one but we need two assistants in addition to myself in the Superintendency, I suggest, President Woodruff, that Brother Heber, here, be made one of the superintendency." And then Brother Roberts was also added.[33]

When President Woodruff asked if he "was willing to work in that capacity," Heber replied in the affirmative. However, he recalled, "I did not tell them I had prayed to the Lord to give me the job."[34]

The *Improvement Era*

The new presidency immediately set about to make needed changes. The year previous a committee assessing the efficacy of Mutual Improvement Associations had "generally conceded that these associations for the spiritual, moral and intellectual uplift of the young men of Zion, were not functioning as perfectly as they should."[35] Priority was given to establishing a new "improvement organ." A new magazine, to be called the *Improvement Era,* was to be edited by Elders Joseph F. Smith and B. H. Roberts, the latter "really responsible for editing the magazine."[36] Heber was named manager, with Thomas Hull appointed as his assistant.

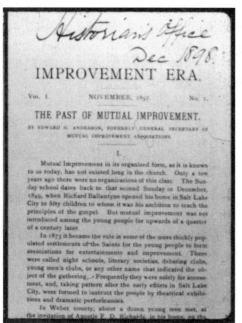

First issue of the *Improvement Era.*
Heber J. Grant was the first business manager and subsequent editor of the magazine.

With the name chosen and the management in place, they lacked only the necessary capital to start such a venture. The recession of 1891 and the depression of 1893 had taxed personal and Church finances alike. Personally the men could contribute little to the cause, and the Church made it clear that it was in no position to aid the project financially. With no means to raise the requisite capital, it appeared that the *Improvement Era* would remain a magazine in name only. However, several on the committee suggested there was yet another source for the money: the would-be readers of the magazine. "Our capital," according to B. H. Roberts, "was the interest of the young men of the Church of Jesus Christ of Latter-day Saints in the Mutual Improvement cause; and that had only to be appealed to, and drawn upon, in order to be sufficient and permanent in the maintenance of the Young Men's organ." It was concluded that "if our case were fittingly presented to the young men of the Church, and our determination to publish such an organ was strong enough, that we could supply the capital by asking our young men for a one year's subscription to the magazine, strictly in advance, and before any numbers were printed at all."[37]

Critics of the plan were not few. How, they wondered, would it be possible to get subscriptions for a magazine that yet did not exist? Solicitations for the *Era* were made by many. Elder Grant and Elder Joseph F. Smith took up the issue in the quarterly conferences they attended. Stake superintendents sought subscriptions, and others, including B. H. Roberts, spent four to six weeks on canvassing missions with each group assigned a specific region to visit. So successful were their efforts that the *Improvement Era*'s first issue was dated November 1897.

As the business manager, Heber worked tirelessly for the magazine's success. One year, for example, he wrote over eight thousand letters seeking donations, subscriptions, or other support for the *Era*. To get the letters out he elicited his family's assistance. Recalling this work, his daughter Lucy suggested, "The *Improvement Era* was almost born in our home—it was at least nurtured there after its birth. Father sent personal letters by the thousands." To these ends the Grant home was transformed into a business office and mailing house. As Lucy described it,

> We had several typewriters and several of us children learned to typewrite getting out *Era* letters. We had a large dining room and an especially large dining room table. This table would be pulled out and half a dozen leaves put in it. Then we would all sit around and some would fold; others would write. Father was usually seated at the end signing his name. We had half a dozen enclosures to put into the envelopes, so it took us all to get these letters ready for the mail.[38]

By July of 1898, Heber was pleased to announce the *Era* already had over five thousand subscriptions.[39]

With the commencement of the third volume in 1899, Heber informed readers that he planned to "become a regular contributor to the columns of the *Era*." Learning that many young men had benefited from his speeches, he wanted "to chat with 'our boys,' as through that medium, I will be able to reach many thousands instead of a few hundred."[40] He also outlined his philosophy of writing: "In contributing to the *Era* a series of articles which will be made up principally of my own experiences, I shall do so, not for the purpose of throwing bouquets at myself, figuratively speaking, but with the hope that I may inspire my readers with a desire to labor."[41] His use of personal stories as illustrations of gospel principles and as examples to follow characterized his approach to writing and speaking throughout his tenure as a General Authority. As a result, the *Era* became a repository for the many life stories that Heber shared over the years, and in conference talks the repetition of these stories was not uncommon.

In addition to the articles containing personal stories, Heber wrote numerous pieces in his capacity as the magazine's manager. He began a May 1912 editorial, for instance, by stating, "As business manager of the *Era,* I wish to thank one and all of its subscribers for their loyal support."[42] Addressing the magazine's purposes at some length, he then concluded with a reminder: "It is the duty of the YMMIA officers to do the work of canvassing, for it is their magazine, and we ask the Priesthood authorities to aid and sustain them, since it is their advocate, too. I now appeal to you, dear reader, to say a good word to or to call on your neighbors with the Mutual workers who are out trying to increase our subscription list." Never one to ask another to do that which he had not done, he asked readers: "Will you do your share? I have signed many hundreds of letters soliciting subscribers—one year as high as 8,000. This on my part has been a labor of love. It would not be necessary for me to do this, and my time could be occupied in something else for the good of the cause, if all our subscribers would do a little, say secure one subscriber each."[43]

One reason for Heber's immense personal investment in the magazine was the contribution he believed it made to missionary work. At a YMMIA conference in June 1931, he told those gathered,

"I do not think I am exaggerating the least particle when I say that the very finest missionary we have in the Church today is the *Improvement Era*." The magazine was to be valued not only for the truths that it taught but also "in providing openings for the elders themselves to deliver their message to people to whom otherwise, perhaps, they would not have gained access."[44] Much of his letter writing focused on raising funds to send issues of the *Era,* free of charge, to the Church's missionaries. In 1897 there were 1,600 missionaries, so $1,600 had to be raised. Heber donated a hundred dollars and then wrote the letters, which he and Joseph F. Smith signed. They received the needed amount plus an additional $1,000. By 1901 Heber reported that "there had been sent to our missionaries over $30,000 worth of *Era*s at the actual cost of the magazine."[45]

Some of the letters sent were later published in the *Era*. Although brief, a necessity in light of how many he mailed out, the letters reveal a bold and determined business manager. To the multimillionaire David Eccles, from whom Heber had previously solicited money on behalf of the Church, Heber wrote:

> Dear Brother Eccles:
> Last year you very kindly gave $100.00 to aid in sending the *Era* free to our Elders who are on missions. I also gave $100.00 last year and have given $75.00 this year. We are short a few hundred dollars on our fund for Volume 2, and if you feel that you would like to aid in this matter I should be pleased to have your check for such amount as you may desire to contribute. I will forward copy of this to Baker City.
> Yours sincerely,
> (Signed) H. J. Grant.

To a bishop in Vernal, Utah, he employed a different strategy: "If you have $25 or $50.00 that you do not know what to do with, and would like to lay up some treasures in Heaven, kindly send it to *The Improvement Era* to be credited to their free missionary account." He concluded the letter by pointing out his own contributions: "$100 for Volume 1, and $75.00 for Volume 2."[46] Coming from some, this statement might have appeared as an unnecessary boast. However, from Heber, it was a simple acknowledgement of the common cause that Church members shared.

Recognizing the contributions of all, Elder Grant did not fail to acknowledge the more humble donations. To Bishop William Thorne in Salt Lake he wrote:

> I am in receipt of two dollars for your subscription to Volume 3, of the *Era*. . . . Please accept of my sincere thanks. . . . I can assure you that it is very much appreciated. We are doing all in our power to make the *Era* . . . a preacher of the gospel. The words of commendation which we are receiving from missionaries to whom the magazine goes free are very gratifying indeed.
> With sincere good wishes for you and yours, I am
> Your friend and brother,
> (Signed) H. J. Grant.[47]

In addition to letters seeking donations and those acknowledging the gifts received, he wrote numerous letters seeking purchasers for the magazine's advertising space.

Heber not only had to sell subscriptions, but he continually had to persuade members to accept his vision of the YMMIA and recognize the program's value. From the beginning, Junius Wells reported, there were naysayers who, despite the prophetic origin of the program, "freely predicted the breaking up of the organization, by the authorities, when they should give it their attention."[48] By 1909, thirty years after the YMMIA was first established, the program was not fully implemented throughout the Church. Out of 685 wards there were still 56 wards that had yet to form an association.[49] As he did often, Grant pleaded with the bishops and stake leadership to make sure that all wards became properly organized. Even subscriptions among association members fell far below what the leadership expected as stakes had difficulty meeting the goal to have 5 percent of stake membership subscribe. Heber had little patience for those who claimed they could not afford the magazine's price of two dollars but would "perhaps spend ten times two dollars for tea, coffee, tobacco or liquor."[50]

Heber ascribed their resistance to a lack of faith. Addressing a general conference audience as the newly called prophet, he chided Church members: "If there is any home in all the Church that does not have the *Era,* it simply shows that the people there are lacking in faith, that they think more of two dollars than they do of getting communications from the authorities of the Church, and important sermons, which are of more value than the things of this world."[51] As for himself, Heber wrote to a friend, "I would not do without the valuable instructions in the *Era* for ten times the price of the subscription. Many complain that they can get a larger eastern paper for less, but this only shows that they do not know how to estimate real value. Life eternal is the pearl of great price that we are after, and little if anything to aid us in securing it is to be found in the eastern magazines, if they do print more matter."[52]

A Lifelong Commitment

For Heber J. Grant, involvement with YMMIA and the *Improvement Era* was truly a life's work. In the very first mutual improvement association he was a charter member and one of its leading officers. He soon thereafter became the Thirteenth Ward president, and when three members of the Twelve were called to lead the organization, Grant became the general secretary. His call first as an assistant to the General Superintendency and then as a counselor to the superintendent reacquainted him with the work. In light of all that he had done, Heber was uniquely qualified to address the topic "The Place of the Young Men's Mutual Improvement Associations in the Church" at a 1912 conference. He outlined clearly the reasons the program existed. To begin with, it was started by Brigham Young, a fact that Heber wanted bishops to remember anytime they announced and sang the hymn "We Thank Thee, O God, for a Prophet." The program also gave "the young men an organization which they can call their own, which young people much desire."[53] And Heber was the opinion that "no greater calamity could befall the young men of this Church than for them to have no organization of their own." Without the associations, he suggested, "we would have large numbers of our young men joining the various secret societies for cheap insurance and sociability."[54] Out of his many years of experience came the belief that "often more practical, good, and more genuine religion can be impressed by a word in the right place, in the games, parties, entertainments, classes and festivals of the young than in much preaching and exhortation." As he did so often he used a personal example to illustrate his point:

> When I was a young man of twenty-four, presiding over the Tooele stake of Zion, passing a baseball game one day, I heard the boys profane. I did not correct them, but I called to one of the players and said: "Next time you have a base-ball game, boys, count me in. I used to play in the nine that won the championship in our territory." The boys did count me in, and I often played with them. The fact that the president of the stake came and played with them was the reason, I think, that no oaths were used in all the games that I played. I never saw finer deportment in my life than those boys exhibited upon the ball field.[55]

The YMMIA provided Church leaders with a regular chance to rub shoulders with the boys in their wards, and Heber hoped all young men in the Church would profit from the associations as he had done.

NOTES TO CHAPTER 7

1. Bryant S. Hinckley, "President Grant—Lover of Youth," *IE,* October 1936, 667.
2. Quoted in Ronald W. Walker, "Young Heber J. Grant's Years of Passage," *BYU Studies* 24 (spring 1984): 144.
3. Autobiography of John Mills Woolley, 31; quoted in Leonard Arrington, *From Quaker to Latter-day Saint: Bishop Edwin D. Woolley* (Salt Lake City: Deseret Book, 1976), 462.
4. Henry W. Naisbitt, "'Polysophical' and 'Mutual,'" *IE,* August 1899, 745.
5. Paul H. Peterson, *The Mormon Reformation* (Provo, Utah: Joseph Fielding Smith Institute for Latter-day History, 2002), 41.
6. Ronald W. Walker, "Growing Up in Early Utah: The Wasatch Literary Association," *Sunstone,* November/December 1981, 44.

7. Orson F. Whitney, "The Wasatch Literary Association," *IE*, September 1925, 1019.
8. Walker, "Growing Up in Early Utah," 47.
9. Ibid., 48.
10. Junius F. Wells, "Historical Sketch of the YMMIA," *IE*, June 1925, 715.
11. Ibid.
12. B. Morris. Young, "Recollections," *IE*, August 1925, 954.
13. Wells, "Historical Sketch of the YMMIA," *IE*, June 1925, 716.
14. Ibid., 717.
15. Wells, "The Original YMMIA," 738.
16. Ibid., 740.
17. Young, "Recollections," 955.
18. Heber J. Grant, as told to Rachel Grant Taylor, "When Brigham Young Watched a Waltz," *IE*, November 1941, 654.
19. Ibid.
20. Ibid.
21. Ibid.
22. Ibid.
23. Ibid.
24. Ibid., 678.
25. Edward H. Anderson, "The Past of Mutual Improvement," *IE*, December 1897, 86.
26. Ibid., 87.
27. Ibid., 85.
28. Ibid., 86.
29. Heber J. Grant, "Growth—How a Living Testimony Endures," *IE*, August 1925, 928.
30. Grant, "The President Speaks to the Youth," *IE*, July 1936, 396.
31. Thomas G. Alexander, *Things in Heaven and Earth: The Life and Times of Wilford Woodruff, a Mormon Prophet* (Salt Lake City: Signature Books, 1993), 311–19.
32. Grant, "The President Speaks to the Youth," 396.
33. Grant, "Growth—How a Living Testimony Endures," 928.
34. Grant, "The President Speaks to the Youth," 396.
35. B. H. Roberts, "The Beginning of the *Improvement Era*, 1897," *IE*, July 1925, 869.

36. Grant, "Growth—How a Living Testimony Endures," 928.
37. Roberts, "The Beginning of the *Improvement Era,* 1897," 870.
38. Hinckley, "President Grant—Lover of Youth," 678.
39. "Our Work," *IE,* July 1898, 700.
40. Grant, "The Nobility of Labor," *IE,* December 1899, 81.
41. Ibid., 82.
42. Grant, "To the Subscribers of the *Era,*" *IE,* May 1912, 648.
43. Ibid., 651.
44. Richard L. Evans, "A Page from the Life of a Business Manager," *IE,* November 1938, 694.
45. Grant, "Growth—How a Living Testimony Endures," 929.
46. Evans, "A Page from the Life of a Business Manager," 665.
47. Ibid.
48. Wells, "Historical Sketch of the YMMIA," *IE,* October 1925, 1152–53.
49. CR, October 1909, 120.
50. Evans, "A Page from the Life of a Business Manager," 694.
51. CR, October 1919, 12.
52. "Our Work," *IE,* December 1906, 153.
53. Grant, "The Place of the Young Men's Mutual Improvement Associations in the Church," *IE,* August 1912, 872.
54. Ibid., 874.
55. Ibid., 877.

～EIGHT～

In 1937, at the age of eighty, President Grant, accompanied by Hugh B. Brown and Joseph Anderson, left Salt Lake City for Quebec, where they sailed to France. During the next three months, Heber visited a dozen countries as he participated in conferences, toured missions, and attended celebrations. He spoke at fifty-five meetings, attended the World Scout Jamboree in Holland, and "was the principal figure at the British Centennial."[1] At the following general conference that fall, Heber reported that they had had no trouble holding meetings in prewar Germany, and he gave an account of their visit to Preston, England, where Heber C. Kimball first preached the gospel in Great Britain a hundred years previous. Of all that President Grant saw and did during this trip there was one thing that stood out above all the rest: "[What] impressed me more profoundly on this mission than anything else was the marvelous change that has come about in the attitude of the people regarding the Latter-day Saints." He found it remarkable that they "had favorable newspaper notices in Germany, Switzerland, Czechoslovakia, in Holland, and in Belgium," and there was "no criticism of any kind . . . just fine notices regarding our meetings." Most noteworthy, at least for Heber, was the response they received in Great Britain, where "the notices in the papers . . . were of such a character that if we had had the privilege of writing them ourselves we could not have written anything that would have pleased us better."[2] The response was a far cry from the defamatory articles commonly published when Heber presided over the European mission some thirty years earlier.

During the sixty-three years that Heber participated in the leading Church counsels, he was witness to a significant transformation in how the Church was perceived. Heber had grown up at a time when the word *Mormon* had come to be synonymous with "all that was absurd in religion, impure in social life, or disloyal to government."[3] Much of the time this opinion was due to the Church's policy on plural marriage. By the time Heber was in his early twenties, the nation had renewed its attack on polygamy. The year Heber was called to the Twelve, 1882, Congress passed the Edmunds Act, which shored up previous anti-polygamy legislation by fixing prison terms for offenders and establishing a five-man commission to enforce the law. As a prominent and visible Mormon, law enforcement set their sights on Heber, and he was charged with unlawful cohabitation on several occasions and arrested once, and his plural wives spent years on the underground. The legal prosecutions in Utah were mirrored by public animosity throughout the nation, which Heber clearly felt on his first trip to New York in the 1880s. "Men would double up their fists," he reported, "and shake them at me saying if they had their way they would put the Mormons in this tabernacle and turn the guns of Fort Douglas upon them."[4] Just a decade later Heber believed that the prejudice that had been "so intense" had "almost entirely died out."[5] Even though this pronouncement in 1893 was clearly premature—the animosity generated by plural marriage was far from over—the years of bad publicity and hatred made the change in public opinion all the more pointed. During his lifetime, Heber J. Grant witnessed remarkable changes in the story that was told about Mormons.

Opposition in Japan

It was in Japan that Heber became an active defender for the Church, as he and his companions faced opposition from the moment they arrived. Prior to their arrival the missionaries—Heber J. Grant, Alma O. Taylor, Horace S. Ensign, and Louis A. Kelsch—made arrangements at a nice hotel that overlooked the town. As they checked in, Heber gave the hotel's proprietor his business card, and when the latter saw the address he commented that he was expecting some preachers from Salt Lake City. "Turn the card over," Heber replied, "and maybe you will find they have arrived." When he examined the card and discovered the preachers were Latter-day Saints, he directly informed them "you cannot stay in my house. I would not let a Mormon sleep under my roof."[6] As the missionaries later found out, several ministers had gotten together and stirred up animosity against the Mormons, petitioning the government not to allow them to preach.

Seeking sympathy for his action, the hotel owner sought out a friend who was editor of an English newspaper and told him what he had done to the Mormons. Rather than give his support, the editor "ripped the man up the back" for refusing board to the Mormons. When Heber later thanked the editor "for his attacking the man for his lack of Christianity and a decent respect for other people," the editor responded in turn: "Don't you bother about thanking me. I have been reading stories about you, and I am going to publish a lot of them." Seeing this pronouncement not as a threat but an opportunity, Heber encouraged him to do so, asking only the privilege of responding to the stories, to which the editor remarked, "You shall

Heber J. Grant (front center) with fellow missionaries to Japan (left to right):
Louis A. Kelsch, Alma O. Taylor, and Horace S. Ensign.

have all the space you want." The editor kept his bargain, and Heber took up his pen in defense of the gospel, writing lengthy articles. The attacks soon abated, Heber surmised, because "the gentleman no doubt concluded that space was too valuable to let me say all that I wanted to say."[7]

Though Heber repeatedly mentioned that he accomplished nothing in Japan, this assessment was more a reflection of his personality and past accomplishments. Though conversions were few in number and poor in quality, by his own admittance, Heber proved to be a capable ambassador for the Church, even if his approach was somewhat out of step with usual missionary practices. As Alma O. Taylor later explained, Heber "spent the early months of his mission in Japan in a dignified environment: the best hostelries were his early headquarters." Such accommodations, though pricey, "made it compatible for the editors of the leading newspapers and magazines to come clamoring for interviews with the 'Mormon' Apostle. The situation attracted and favorably impressed government officials and cultural leaders."[8] This positive reception was instrumental in getting government permission to proselytize in the country.

For Heber proselytizing was greatly hampered by his inability to learn the language. Try as he did, he made little progress despite hours of study. However, his ambassadorial role continued throughout his mission, as he was "busy all the time, talking with those that called upon me, answering letters."[9] He spent time attempting to counter the falsities spread about the Church. One article published against the Latter-day Saints included a statement from a sermon by Brigham Young in which he announced, "We have in our midst the biggest liars, the meanest devils that ever walked on the face of the earth."[10] Heber procured the complete sermon and took it to the paper's editor, requesting he publish the statement in context, but he was flatly refused.

Countering the negative publicity, Elder Grant wrote his own tract announcing the missionaries' intentions. Though firm in declaring his belief in Jesus Christ and His gospel, Heber's writings were clearly defensive as he anticipated his audience's initial rejection of the missionaries' teachings. Thus he tried to outline how individuals ought to investigate their message. The Mormons, Heber argued, should be judged "by their fruits" and not by the "false statements of [their] enemies."[11] He emphasized the need to be "fair" and to have an "unprejudiced mind," the antithesis, at least according to Heber, of the way Mormonism was typically treated.[12] The tract is telling in that it reveals how Heber saw his missionary calling; he was not only to bear testimony but he had to break down prejudice and overcome the prevailing negative publicity. He was not only a preacher but an educator; he was there to tell a different story of Mormonism than the one people had previously heard.

Elder Grant also became involved in another critical publishing effort when he met Goro Takanhashi, a leading Christian apologist in Japan. The latter had written an article criticizing the bad press given to the Latter-day Saints and the general opposition shown to them, and Heber invited him to dinner at his hotel. Following the meal, Takanhashi offered to write a book in defense of the Church. Heber provided him with numerous volumes on the Church, and they discussed the project at length. When Heber returned to Salt Lake City in April 1902 for general conference, he spent a good portion of his talk discussing the forthcoming book, going so far as to read headings for the ten chapters. Elder Grant told the Saints, "I feel that this man was raised up of God to do this, and although he may have made some mistakes I believe his book will do us a great deal of good."[13] One suspects the focus on Takanhashi's work in this address was because it was one tangible accomplishment in what otherwise had been a very difficult assignment for Heber.

When he next spoke at conference, in October 1903, Elder Grant gave a report on the year and a half he spent in Japan. In part he praised Horace Ensign, one of the original missionaries who would now lead the mission. Commenting on the difficulty of the work, Heber suggested, "One reason perhaps why Brother Ensign got a bit discouraged at times was . . . because he had had such an active, energetic life as a missionary in Colorado. There he was at it early and late, singing, praying and preaching, outdoors and indoors; then to go over to Japan, sit down and study what people call 'that abominable language' day after day, with nothing else to do—well, I tell you it takes a whole lot more courage and endurance than it does to get out and do active work. It tests a man more than it does to labor."[14] While this was a description of Brother Ensign, the statement was also clearly autobiographical. For the ever-achieving Heber, who regularly accomplished what he set out to do, the work in Japan was advancing slowly, and he had little to show for his enormous efforts.

A Call to England

Elder Grant's frustrations with his calling in Japan were compounded by what he perceived to be a lack of direction from the Spirit. He told Alma Taylor that "he never once felt sure, with that sureness which the clear witness of the Spirit gives, that any given decision or plan was right."[15] Exasperated with the situation in Japan, Heber sought a change in the field of his labors. As he explained,

> Realizing that I was accomplishing little or nothing in spreading the gospel in that nation, I went out into the woods, knelt down and told God that I knew of no man who was more energetic as a missionary, who would organize and plan and put a mission in better shape than Francis M. Lyman; that he would fill up all the mud-holes, so to speak; that he would go along quietly and orderly, laboring for the salvation of the people; that he would build a strong, splendid road on which a man could travel rapidly, if he so desired. *I told him I loved to go fast.*[16]

Almost immediately Elder Grant received word from President Joseph F. Smith to return to Salt Lake where he received a call to follow Lyman as president of the European mission.

In reporting on his labors in Japan, Heber had no problems admitting, even emphasizing his failures. In speaking to the Saints in October 1903, he explained, "I know that the Latter-day Saints have been greatly interested in the mission I was called to preside over, and I regret I am not able to tell you that we have done something wonderful over in Japan. To be perfectly frank with you, I acknowledge I have accomplished very little indeed, as the president of that mission." Reporting his hesitancy at returning home, he commented that "I disliked to have to tell you that I had been there 15 months and done nothing."[17] Although he may have overstated them to some degree, Heber did not mind acknowledging his shortcomings.

Heber arrived in England with his wife Emily and six daughters at the end of 1903, and he assumed leadership of the mission in January 1904. What was originally to be a yearlong assignment was extended for an extra two years, as Heber and family did not return home until December 1906. In stark contrast to the account of his previous work in Japan, Heber later wrote, "In all my labors I got nearer to the Lord and had more joy in the mission field than ever before or since, and the joy I experienced in the mission field was superior to any I have experienced elsewhere."[18] Clearly Heber enjoyed going fast.

Although accustomed to hard work, he found himself working even harder in this new assignment. He wrote, "I can truthfully say that I have never worked more hours in my life per day than I have since I arrived in Liverpool."[19] Elder Grant enjoyed interacting with the numerous elders, preaching extensively, and visiting the Saints in the mission. His enthusiasm never waned, though baptisms were modest given the expansive territory covered by the mission. (It stretched from Norway to South Africa; Elder Grant, however, primarily presided over the British Isles and traveled to Holland, Scandinavia, Germany and Switzerland.)[20] One elder described his president by saying, "He was a veritable dynamo of enthusiasm for placing the Gospel before the people."[21]

As mission president, Heber was responsible for printing, having printed, and distributing an enormous amount of Church literature. As one missionary recalled, "The amount of literature distributed during his administration had never before been equaled. It was turned out of the *Millennial Star* office by the tons."[22] Concerning this work, Heber wrote, "I rejoiced . . . in the wonderful sowing of seeds of truth by distributing millions upon millions of pages of the writings of Charles W. Penrose, during the last year of my administration there."[23] His efforts proved to be a wonderful introduction to the man who succeeded him as president, and in that final year four million tracts were printed and distributed.[24]

The tracts distributed were a means of countering the bad press the Church received during Heber's tenure in Liverpool. Coinciding with hearings about Reed Smoot's election to Congress, the Mormons and plural marriage once again became fodder for the British press. Even Heber was targeted by the newspapers as he had left Salt Lake hastily to avoid charges for unlawful cohabitation.[25] As he had done in Japan, Heber sought space in the papers to refute the untruths, distortions, and slanderous tales. However, when he visited the offices of a paper that "had published seven to ten columns . . . of vile misrepresentations about us," Heber discovered the British editors were not accommodating.[26] Speaking with the paper's assistant editor, Heber told him "it would be a great pleasure to me if he would allow me to write a reply in refutation of the many vile and wicked falsehoods that had been published in his paper regarding the Church." When he was told the truth had already been published, Heber pulled from his briefcase a cache of letters from non-Mormon bankers from across the United States all vouching for his honesty. "I defy you," he challenged the editor, "to get a letter of recommendation from some responsible person, vouching for any individual who has furnished you these falsehoods." The editor was little impressed by the letters of support and flatly denied the request. "Never mind what you assure me," he said. "We will not publish anything you have to say."[27]

Not one to give up easily, Heber was not about to leave meekly. As turned to leave, he asked the man,

> "Is your name Robinson?"
> "Yes."
> "Are you related to Phil Robinson?"
> "Oh, no."
> "Do you know Phil Robinson?"
> "Do I know Phil Robinson? Everybody knows Phil Robinson."
> "Well I am glad to know that. Was he the correspondent of the London Daily Telegraph during the Boer War, one of the two greatest of all the London papers?" . . .
> "Yes, he was."
> "And would you believe anything and everything he wrote?"
> "I would."

To the last reply, Heber challenged him to read Robinson's *Sinners and Saints* written about the reporter's travels in Utah. "If you will buy that book, sir, you will find that everything you have said in your paper is a malicious falsehood."[28] Taken aback by Heber's persistence, the editor relented and suggested he could have half a column for his refutation. The article was accepted but never published, and it was sent back a couple of months later with a note indicating that space in paper could not be found for the piece.

Not all of Heber's efforts to tell an accurate story of Mormonism were rebuffed, and "with several elders providing copy, [he] managed to place several items with the press."[29] As the ranking Church leader in England, Elder Grant became almost excessively anxious about the Church's image. He spent a great deal of time, money, and other resources distributing tracts, speaking in defense of the Church, and trying to get articles published in the newspapers.

On his missions, a new side of Heber J. Grant that had perhaps lain latent prior to this time was born; he became a defender of the faith. Not content to allow others to slander as they would, Heber answered as many challenges to his faith as he possibly could. His strong testimony combined with memories of stories his mother had told him about the persecutions of the early days of the Church no

Heber J. Grant, president of the European mission, accompanied by missionaries in Britain. Daughters, Edith and Grace, are seated to Heber's left.

doubt left the young man eager to stand amongst the people of the world and proclaim the truth of what he believed. His first extended opportunity to do so outside of Utah came during his missions as he increasingly faced the negative view so much of the world had of his people. Not willing to simply proclaim his beliefs, he felt he must answer every attack that he could.

A Prophet Answers Critics and Acknowledges Tributes

When Heber J. Grant became the President of the Church on 23 November 1918, four days following the death of President Joseph F. Smith, he continued the practice of responding to critics. During his conference addresses he regularly discussed how the Church was perceived by both friend and foe. Often he acknowledged what critics of the Church and of himself had said and refuted their claims. And typically his responses were anything but reserved. In his opening address at the October 1922 conference he read a newspaper article that had been sent to him. He prefaced his reading by suggesting, "I thought the annexed clipping would be information to you, as it was to me." The article, entitled "Mormon Leader Political Boss Says Reformer," claimed, "Today H. J. Grant patronizes presidents, makes bargains with great political parties, dictates the political policies of Utah and at least five surrounding states and wields effective political influences in at least five others." Again President Grant was quick to discredit both content and the article's author. "The gentleman must have been listening to one of the lying speeches of a notorious anti-'Mormon' woman. Martin is the Superintendent of the National Reform Association. If he is properly quoted he better reform himself, and purge himself of falsehood." Heber then used the story to further link himself with the prophets that came before him. "Joseph Smith was told that his name 'should be had for good and evil among all nations,' or that it should be both 'good and evil spoken of among all people,' and we, his successors, have had the same privilege."[30] For Heber J. Grant, and for many Mormons, the bad press was evidence of divine favor.

Not only concerned with altering how outsiders saw the Church, he was also very attentive to what story the Mormons told about themselves. In 1911, then a member of the Twelve, he recalled reading an article critical of the Church in the *North American Review*. Written by a grandson of Brigham Young, Heber attacked the article by attacking the author. A firm believer in the scriptural passage "by their fruits ye shall know them," Heber announced that "no young man in all Israel has made a more unsavory record; no young man in all Israel has been more guilty of bringing sorrow and pain and humiliation to his parents; no young man has been more guilty of lying about the servants of God than this same man who today is publishing attacks upon the Latter-day Saints." Comparing the man with his half-brother Richard Young provided evidence enough for why these opinions ought to be discounted. Though Heber did not provide evidence for his assertion, he declared, "I rejoice in knowing that [such articles] are false."[31] In responding to critics Heber certainly didn't hesitate to go on the offensive, acknowledging disparagement with his own condemnation.

President Grant spent a significant portion of one conference speech providing a line-by-line rebuttal to an article commenting primarily on the financial affairs of the Church. Among the many claims, though, the author of the article asserted that despite public denials, plural marriage was still taught by leading Church authorities. As was so often the case, the evidence President Grant provided was his own testimony, setting up an intended contrast between his credibility and that of the person to whom he was responding.

> In spite of all falsehoods by liars—I thought I wouldn't use that word, but really a liar is a liar, and perhaps once in a while it is wise to say so—in spite of every document printed, in spite of every statement to the contrary by any person on the face of the earth, the Authorities of this Church under the administration of Heber J. Grant as President, have never taught, have never encouraged, have never sustained any human being in entering pretended plural marriage. All these statements are pure and simple falsehoods.[32]

After several minutes of reading and responding, Heber commented, "I did intend to comment on a full half column, but I really think it is a waste of breath."³³ Certainly the audience may have questioned why, if it was a waste of breath, he had begun in the first place. Even with his own ambiguity on taking the time in conference to address critics, however, the prevalence of these responses—the corrections of lies told about them—in his speeches clearly indicate that Heber felt it important to provide the Saints with an official position.

While always ready to respond to the critics, Heber spent just as much time in his talks, if not more, recognizing the increasing number of tributes paid to the Mormons. Even early in his service in the Quorum of the Twelve, he used reports of such favorable opinions as the basis for talks. On several occasions he read a personal letter from a "man of considerable experience and importance in the business world" who was not a Church member. "Many times," the man wrote, "and oft I have said, in conversation, that the only religious people I ever knew who lived up to their professions, were the Mormons of Utah. And this is true." As Heber was never one to let an opportunity go by to make a point, he added after reading the letter, "I am indeed grateful that my friend has not access to the list of non-tithe-payers, amounting to ten thousand."³⁴ Heber marveled that a man of such standing, and one who was an admitted agnostic, could hold the Mormons in such high esteem. Though the newspapers made it seem like the world was all against them, Heber felt it important to acknowledge that was not the case.

As prophet, President Grant repeatedly commented in speeches on the "most wonderful change in the attitude of the people of the world toward the Latter-day Saints."³⁵ In 1920, during the first April conference after becoming President of the Church, he gave a lengthy address largely consisting of recent adulations the Mormons had been given in Congress.³⁶ Following a speech by Utah senator Reed Smoot, a senator from Arizona had gotten up and acknowledged how the Mormon "church has elevated many intellects and purified many hearts in my State," and a Colorado senator paid tribute to the Mormons' "morality and usefulness," praising the loyalty they demonstrated to their country. President Grant read a transcript of these speeches along with the comments made by a Nevada senator. These compliments echoed the ones Heber heard as he traveled throughout the United States. As he told the Saints, "Our character is becoming known, and no longer can men lie about the Latter-day Saints, or women either, and get away with the lies with the great majority of the people in our country."[37] The lies and slander of years previous were slowly giving way to praise and respect.

The change in public opinion resulted in opportunities that before would have been unfathomable. During a trip to Washington, Heber J. Grant cordially met with members of the president's cabinet, senators and representatives, and officials from the Federal Reserve.[38] Several years later, President Grant even announced to a conference audience that he had had the pleasure of playing a round of golf with the president of the United States. Particularly symbolic of the change in how Mormonism was perceived was a request President Grant received to address three hundred influential businessmen in Kansas City. He spoke of the "hardships, the drivings and the persecutions" that early Mormons had faced. Most remarkable was the response he received: "To have that body of representative men receive that address with approval, applaud it in many places, and many of them come to me after the meeting and shake hands and congratulate me upon the address" was noteworthy given the proximity to Independence, Missouri.[39] Mormonism had indeed come a long way.

Commenting on the positive press was a regular part of President Grant's speeches. In 1927 he told the Saints, "I find no difficulty whatever in getting publicity in the various papers; and when I travel, in different cities in the east and west, the north or the south, those who have interviewed me have given correct reports of the interviews." He was particularly impressed with the "splendid publicity in the European papers" that Elder James E. Talmage was receiving. When he reported on the Arizona Temple dedication, he commented, as would be expected, on the "rich outpouring of the Spirit" that was felt. Almost as quickly, though, he acknowledged "the remarkable publicity that was given to us by the newspapers of Arizona," which was grounds for "rejoic[ing] exceedingly."[40] The changing story told about the Church had had a most profound effect on Heber.

The President Speaks in Michigan

Indicative of the increasing public respect given to President Grant and the Church was the invitation to speak at the Second

Heber J. Grant with Henry Ford.

Dearborn Conference of Agriculture, Industry, and Science sponsored by the Chemical Foundation and Farm Chemurgic Council. The three-day conference, which was attended by 1,200 "leading scientists, industrial executives, and agricultural leaders," was held with the stated goal "to advance the industrial use of American farm products through applied science."[41] President Grant confessed to the press upon entering the conference, "I know little of what these men are doing," adding that he was there to "learn and tell something of our sugar industry in Utah."[42]

On the first night, Heber was one of several who addressed the conference. As he began his address he surely recognized the irony of his opening statement: "I am sure that the principal reason for my being invited to make a speech here this evening is that I stand at the head of the Church of Jesus Christ of Latter-day Saints, commonly known as the Mormon Church."[43] Whereas for decades the word *Mormon* had been to many a term of disdain, and Church presidents were considered tyrannical threats to American society, President Grant had been selected to speak not because of his technical expertise but because of his respected Church position. Moving through his subjects at a brisk pace, Heber gave an introduction to Brigham Young's settlement of the West. He mentioned, but did not belabor, the persecutions Mormons suffered prior to arriving in the Salt Lake Valley. As he was wont to do in any speech, experiences from his life were included to personalize the topic and make his points. He told of his earliest encounter with Brigham Young as he hitched a ride on the prophet's sleigh, and he related the challenges faced in raising money for the sugar factory. Recounting stories that general conference goers would readily recognize, he extolled the virtues of Young's emphasis on self-reliance.

A lengthy introduction was followed by a history of the sugar industry in Utah, starting with John Taylor's importing the needed machinery in the 1850s. He detailed the decision to restart the industry in the late 1880s and outlined the financial benefits the state had reaped as a consequence. Like most speeches he gave, Heber was bold in his opinions: "To my mind it is a poor financial policy to buy from any foreign country anything that can be profitably produced by the tiller of the soil in the United States, and especially is this the case with something as profitable as sugar." And the speech was peppered with tangential statements: "You will pardon me for announcing that the leading officials of the Mormon Church have requested the members of the Church who are in good standing to discontinue receiving relief from the government, except in cases where wages are paid for services rendered." He concluded by acknowledging the Mormon Church's tendency to have older leaders, and though he was nearly eighty, he pointed out that "age is a quality of mind."[44]

A Church member in attendance reported that at the end of President Grant's speech the audience "rose to their feet and applauded long and enthusiastically," in contrast to the "moderate applause" given to other speakers that evening.[45] Some in the audience were heard to say, "That was worth coming from New York to hear," and "I'd go a hundred miles any day to hear that kind of talk."[46] It was observed that "from that moment until President Grant left Detroit for home, he was the center of attention and easily the outstanding and most talked of personality at the conference." At a banquet the second night, President Grant received an unexpected request to speak yet again. In introducing him, the toastmaster for the evening announced, "Ladies and gentlemen: In response to many requests from all over the hall I have been able to induce one of our guests to give you the great treat of hearing from him once more at this conference. I know that every one of you knows whom I mean (applause); a young blade from out West, who has brought to us inspiration, relaxation, enjoyment, and now anticipation drifts into the realm. I beg to introduce President Heber J. Grant."[47]

When he got to the podium, President Grant thanked this audience for the applause and made explicit the source of his great pleasure: "It might interest you people to know that I spent three years in

Europe and that during that entire three years I was not able to get one line in the newspaper in refutation of some of the most libelous attacks upon the people that I represent."[48] When he returned to his hotel that night, Heber had difficulty sleeping due to the joy he felt.

> When I retired that night, I was unable to sleep for many hours because of the gratitude that filled my heart for the wonderful change that had come about in the attitude of the world at large toward our people. When I thought of the persecutions and trials and tribulations of our people; when I thought of my own mother being rejected by her brothers and cast out as a thing of evil; when I thought of laboring in England for three long years, during which time some of the most wicked and vile and devilish things imaginable were printed in the newspapers about our people, . . . and then when I thought of the great body of leading men of the greatest, if not the very greatest, financial men in our country applauding my remarks that were practically telling of the accomplishments of the Church, and applauding them to the echo, it was impossible for me to sleep.

It was experiences like these that led him to later assert, "The railing out against the Church, the viciousness and the lying about our people as a whole have almost entirely died out because people have come to know the desires of our hearts."[49] Certainly Heber J. Grant deserved some of the credit for the change. As a boy he had worked for and with non-Mormons.[50] As a successful businessman he cooperated well with people not of the Church to promote the business affairs of Salt Lake.[51] And as a member of the Twelve he believed in the "basic virtue of political, economic, and social cooperation with non-Mormons."[52] He had made it a policy to never shy away from those not of his faith. Rather he had always sought out opportunities to make himself and the Church known to those who did not believe as he did. In this regard, Heber was both a reporter of and instrument in changing how the Church was perceived by outsiders.

NOTES TO CHAPTER 8

1. Richard L. Evans, "The President's Year in Thirteen Nations," *IE,* April 1938, 204.
2. CR, October 1937, 8.
3. B.H. Roberts, *The Life of John Taylor* (Salt Lake City: Bookcraft, 1963; second collector's edition, 1994), 249.
4. CR, April 1936, 9.
5. *Collected Discourses,* 3:373.
6. CR, October 1936, 10.
7. Ibid., 11.
8. Alma O. Taylor, "Memories of Far-Off Japan: President Grant's First Foreign Mission, 1901 to 1903," *IE,* November 1936, 690.
9. CR, April 1902, 46.
10. CR, April 1909, 114.
11. Heber J. Grant, "An Announcement Concerning the Church of Jesus Christ of Latter-day Saints," *IE,* July 1903, 713.
12. Ibid., 714.
13. CR, April 1902, 49.
14. CR, October 1903, 11.
15. Taylor, "Memories of Far-Off Japan," 691.
16. Grant, "Growth—How a Living Testimony Endures," *IE,* August 1925, 929–30; emphasis added.
17. CR, October 1903, 7, 11.
18. Grant, "Greetings from Across the Sea," *IE,* July 1937, 405.
19. Grant to George Teasdale, 18 January 1906; quoted in Ronald W. Walker, "Heber J. Grant's European Mission, 1903–1906," *Journal of Mormon History* 14 (1988): 20.
20. Walker, "Heber J. Grant's European Mission, 1903–1906," 17, 24.
21. R. Eugene Allen, "The Mission President in Europe," *IE,* November 1936, 694.
22. Ibid., 694–95.
23. Grant, "Growth—How a Living Testimony Endures," 930.
24. Walker, "Heber J. Grant's European Mission, 1903–1906," 20.
25. Ibid.
26. CR, April 1932, 7.
27. CR, October 1936, 8.

28. Ibid., 9.

29. Walker, "Heber J. Grant's European Mission, 1903–1906," 22.

30. CR, October 1922, 8.

31. CR, April 1911, 22.

32. CR, April 1932, 121.

33. Ibid., 122.

34. CR, April 1901, 31.

35. CR, April 1927, 6.

36. While Heber J. Grant had been called as President in November 1918, the 1919 April conference had been postponed to June because of a flu epidemic.

37. CR, April 1920, 7, 9, 12.

38. Ibid., 12.

39. CR, April 1921, 7.

40. CR, April 1928, 7.

41. Stringham A. Stevens, "The President Goes to Dearborn," *IE,* July 1936, 397.

42. Ibid., 399.

43. Grant, "A Domestic Sugar Supply," *IE,* September 1936, 523.

44. Ibid., 525, 525–26, 526.

45. Stevens, "The President Goes to Dearborn," 398, 397.

46. Ibid., 398.

47. Grant, "A Domestic Sugar Supply," 526.

48. Ibid.

49. CR, October 1939, 43–44.

50. Grant, "Some Things for Our Young People to Remember," *IE,* July 1939, 393. As Heber explained, "I entered an office as a young man fifteen years of age and I labored among those not of our faith until I engaged in business for myself at nineteen. Then I was connected with institutions at home and abroad, none of which were Mormon institutions—companies in England, France, Germany, from New York to San Francisco. All of my contacts in a business way were with those not of our faith."

51. Thomas G. Alexander, *Things in Heaven and Earth: The Life and Times of Wilford Woodruff, a Mormon Prophet* (Salt Lake City: Signature Books, 1993), 283.

52. Ibid., 268.

~ NINE ~

Heber's description of himself as "long and lanky" applied throughout his life. At six feet tall he weighed a mere 140 pounds. Even when he succeeded, on a few occasions, in putting on weight, it would be difficult to consider him anything but notably thin. Just as it had been a liability when he began playing baseball, his lean stature proved to be a problem later in life. Ever concerned with his mother's financial future, Heber as a young man sought to purchase life insurance for himself. It was with some irony that the burgeoning insurance salesman could not purchase the desired policy. The doctors who examined him were sure that his frail body would succumb easily to disease, and were he to contract pneumonia, they believed, it would certainly kill him. Although he spent several months bedridden with pneumonia following his operation for appendicitis, he took great pleasure in proving the doctors wrong. "Some years ago," he told a congregation of Saints in 1898, "I tried to insure my life, but the companies refused. Their physicians told me that if I ever took pneumonia I would die. But I am still here, notwithstanding the report of the physicians of the life insurance companies."[1] Though frail, Heber proved to be quite resilient.

Throughout his life Heber J. Grant faced a variety of health challenges of varying severity. With his call as stake president and his move to Tooele, Heber faced many challenges that took their toll on his health.[2] Heber's previous Church experience left him unprepared to be a proficient preacher, and he was not ready to provide the ministerial guidance his stake members always needed. His youngest daughter contracted an illness that nearly proved fatal, and his wife Lucy began to suffer from stomach problems that ultimately did prove fatal. Compounding these problems was the precarious position of his finances. Following a fire that destroyed his vinegar plant in Ogden, Heber worked long hours to pay the debts incurred. All this stress exacted a price, and he "almost yielded to 'nervous convulsions.'"[3] This nervous breakdown brought warnings from his doctor that he must slow down or he would experience a "softening of the brain."[4]

In addition to being concerned about his frail nerves, Heber suffered from insomnia throughout his life. At one point, he was "ordered to leave town within twenty-four hours or I might go crazy for lack of sleep." He went to California where he found he "could sleep there three or four nights in succession, twelve hours at a time without waking up."[5]

For the most part, the insomnia was only a disruption in his life, and he learned how to be productive in spite of the condition. "I learned to sing a song or two, or three, or four, or five, as high as ten when I would wake up, and then to get up and take some physical exercises, and take some in bed, and try to go to sleep, and failing, sit up and talk to a Dictaphone for an hour, and then go back to sleep."[6] While president of the European mission, he got to the point where he could not sleep past three or four in the morning. To compensate he began take short naps in the afternoon that helped him make it through the day.[7] He often used these early mornings to get a jump on the day's work. It was not uncommon for letters dictated by President Grant to be accompanied by a statement such as "it is now 4 A.M. and I have been dictating two hours."[8] Although later in life he happily announced that he had experienced "only two severe attacks of insomnia since I returned over thirty years ago from Europe,"[9] the insomnia was particularly difficult in his final years.

As a result of his lifestyle, personality, and health conditions, Heber J. Grant's appearance belied his actual age. An incident which clearly demonstrated how he had aged prematurely took place at the end of his mission in England when he was fifty years old. One evening his wife Emily wanted to go to the theater but Heber was so tired he replied, "I wouldn't go to the finest theater on the face of the earth. I am tired. I am going to bed to rest and sleep." He suggested that his wife find a missionary to take her and her daughters and use the tickets they had been given. Elder Charles W. Penrose, who had just arrived to take Heber's place as mission president, offered to take the women. "Sister Grant," he said, "let the old man go to bed; I will take you to the theater." The next day, a mover bringing furniture into the new mission home was asked to guess the age of the two Apostles. Heber later recalled:

> He looked us over carefully, and he said, "I should say that Mr. Grant is sixty-five, and that Mr. Penrose is sixty."
>
> I said, "I have heard that a man is no older than he feels, and a woman no older than she looks. I felt so old that I went to bed last night because I was tired, and this old man here, twenty-five years older than I am—so, you have only made a mistake of thirty years—took my wife and daughters to the theater."
>
> The next Sunday I thought that I would get that corrected. . . . While at Birmingham I asked the president of the branch who he thought was older, Brother Penrose or myself—expecting to have a correct answer—and he said, "The idea of asking such a ridiculous question; anybody can see you are very much older than Brother Penrose." I hit the table, and said, "That settles it, no old man will ever take my wife to the theater again," and he never has.[10]

Though not necessarily athletic, Heber was always energetic. As a young boy he retired from baseball after his team won the territory championship, and he largely gave up sports until his mission in England, when he became smitten with tennis.[11] A tennis court was installed in the backyard of the mission home, and according to one daughter, he "played all he could, between conferences, meetings, and trips."[12] He justified the time spent playing in terms of the health benefit it provided. "I eat and sleep much better by taking this pleasure. Physical exercise by using dumb bells may be equally as beneficial but it certainly is very annoying to me."[13] Later in life, at the behest of his doctor, Heber pursued outdoor exercise by learning to play golf. He quickly became an avid golfer, and one report indicated that President Grant "enjoys a rather steady diet of golf and plays a skillful game which expresses itself in low scores."[14] Heber also enjoyed the outdoors, and he regularly went for scenic drives. At one conference, he reported climbing Mt. Timpanogos (11,750 feet) with his son-in-law. "From the top of that mountain, the view of Wasatch, Utah, and Salt Lake counties, the cities therein, and other sections of the country in the distance, is one of the grandest that my eyes have ever beheld."[15] Heber was nearly seventy years old at the time.

Heber's health seemed to get better as he advanced in age, and he gained a vigor that had escaped him in his earlier years. In 1931, in his second decade as President of the Church, he noted in his journal, "I have excellent health, and attribute part of it to the fact that for several years past I have seldom missed a day without taking exercise unless I had the privilege of playing a game of golf."[16] A year later at the April conference he acknowledged the good health he enjoyed: "It may sound a little egotistical, but few men reach the age of seventy-five years in perfect vigor of health of body and mind."[17] Even at age eighty he continued to work eight to nine hours a day, telling the Saints, "I do not ask any man or child in this Church, although I will be eighty years of age next month, to work any more hours than I do."[18] At the Dearborn conference that same year, many of the reporters commented on his physical vitality and mental astuteness. In contrast with accounts of the middle-aged Grant, the reporters wrote: "Erect, vigorous, and bearded, Grant belies his great age."[19]

When his responsibilities as President began to take their toll on the aging prophet, J. Reuben Clark, President Grant's First Counselor, gave instructions to General Authorities and other Church leaders in April 1938 to "avoid taxing the energies of President Grant."[20] Despite slowing down somewhat, President Grant remained active for an octogenarian. On a trip to San Diego at the beginning of 1940, he spoke at the dedication of the Mormon Battalion Monument while also finding time to play several rounds of golf with friends. During the last round he shot a 45, which he acknowledged was the "the best game for a long time I have played."[21] On 4 February he attended a stake conference in Los Angeles. Just prior to the morning session, he suffered a dizzy spell and stumbled to the ground. Although he declined to speak that morning, he gave a lengthy discourse in the afternoon session. The dizziness returned the following morning, and President Grant was taken to the hospital; he had suffered a stroke, which paralyzed his left side and impaired his speech. So severe was the stroke that some feared he would never regain use of his left arm and leg, and the left side of his face was notably disfigured—as he observed, "one of my eyes was crooked; and . . . my mouth was twisted."[22] Though he initially made great strides in recovering and gained some of his strength back, the progress was not permanent.

Although the stroke would greatly hinder him for the rest of his life, the conference addresses he gave in the five years before his death reveal the same indomitable spirit that he had always demonstrated. The following excerpts from these conference talks tell the story of President Grant's last years and show the determination, perseverance, work ethic, and sense of humor that were ever present as he counseled the Saints.

April Conference 1940

The following telegram from President Grant was read by President J. Reuben Clark Jr.:

Los Angeles, California April 5, 1940
Presidents J. Reuben Clark Jr. and David O. McKay, Salt Lake City, Utah,
To the Saints in Conference assembled: I sincerely regret that I am not present with you at this opening meeting of our Conference. I know of the spiritual uplift that will come to you. Through the years I have always counted it a great blessing to participate with my brethren and sisters in General Conference.

The telegram went to explain some of the details surrounding his illness and briefly summarized his recovery. Never one to just sit back and take it easy, President Grant had "hoped at least to speak to the Conference by radio," but to his dismay "the doctors feel it unwise to subject myself to that great strain." He did look forward to when he could return to Salt Lake in "another few weeks."[23]

October Conference 1940

> It is needless for me to tell you good people how grateful I am to be here today. I missed the Conference six months ago, and I am grateful beyond expression to all of you good people, to the Saints generally, and to some people who are not members of our Church for your and their faith and prayers in my behalf that I should be healed. I am grateful to the doctors who so kindly, carefully, and energetically at home, and while in Los Angeles, gave me the benefit of their services.[24]

Although back to conference only six months later, President Grant was certainly not back to normal. Gone were his days of playing golf, and he had significant difficulties singing. As he told the Saints at this conference, he even had to alter his usual method of preaching: "As a rule I never put my remarks on paper, but my mind is not working as well the last five or six months as usual, and I therefore asked my secretary, Brother Anderson, to copy quite a number of things that I know off by heart, at least I did before my illness, but I do not know whether I know them today or not, so I am going to read to you."[25]

One thing that did not change was his sense of humor. In telling the Saints the many personal stories, he never shied away from laughing at himself. Years before, as a junior member of the Twelve, he admonished the Saints to read, study, and ponder the gospel, and he admitted he had to make a special effort to do so because was not "naturally a student." Rather, as he explained, "my mind reaches out for the material things of this kingdom." To emphasize his point he quoted a Salt Lake newspaper which suggested that "Heber J. Grant's favorite song is 'We Thank Thee, O God for a Prophet,' and that he spells it 'p-r-o-f-i-t.'"[26] Continuing with the self-deprecating humor after the stroke, he told a conference audience, "I am perfectly willing to go along as slowly as the Lord wants, but the quicker I get so that I can talk faster and get more accustomed to these false teeth, the better I will like it. (Laughter.)"[27]

October Conference 1941

> The doctor gave me only twenty minutes, but I have concluded to take a lot more than twenty minutes. By not speaking loud I do not believe it will hurt me; I hope not at least. I have been asked for a year and a half, in fact a little longer than that, "How do you feel?" I have said, "Better than yesterday," and I believe it is true, but the improvement has been limited, and I am not yet in good health. Judging from the newspapers one would think I was in first class condition, but they overdid it.

Although limited physically, Heber had a hard time slowing down; it simply wasn't in his nature. Only a year and a half after his stroke, he had convinced his doctors to allow him to spend two and a half hours a day at his office working. However, he easily overdid it on occasions. He attended a banquet at Brigham Young University one evening and commencement exercises the following day. Though he tried to make up for lost sleep by resting in the car on the way home, his doctor was none too pleased by his exertion, and he "got a sentence of ten days in bed."[28] Even in speaking at this conference, he was not to be restrained. Although his doctor wanted him to speak for only twenty minutes at the opening session, he spoke forty. Then at evening session he talked for another forty-seven minutes, which was followed by brief addresses on Sunday.

October Conference 1942

> I am grateful beyond my power of expression for the faith and prayers of the people and for the blessings of the Lord in my behalf. For two and one-half years I have been gaining a little since I became ill. I have been home since that illness overtook me a little longer than two years, and when people have asked me how I am, I have said, "Better than I was yesterday," and this is really true—I have been gaining a little all the time.[29]

In the intervening years, Heber had made notable improvements. As he reported, "To start with I could not raise a finger on my left hand, neither could I touch my chin; my left eye was affected, also my left leg, necessitating me to go upstairs one step at a time, and then lift the other leg up with my right hand. I can now throw my left arm any way I want to, and can go up and down stairs without difficulty. I am feeling at least a hundred percent, if not several hundred percent better than I did at the time of my first trouble."[30] His assessment would ultimately prove overly optimistic, and he would be unable in the remaining years to give his conference addresses, which had to be read by others.

October Conference 1943

It is not thought safe by the doctor for me to make a talk of any length at the conference, so I have decided merely to thank the Saints for their faith and prayers in my behalf, and to assure them I am gaining a little all the time. I hope that by the next conference I may be able to address the Saints at greater length.[31]

At times, as his secretary, Joseph Anderson, reported, President Grant was able to come "to the office nearly every day for a short time and [sign] the mail that had been prepared by his counselors for the First Presidency, also missionary calls and letters pertaining to missionary work."[32] But increasingly he missed the meetings of the First Presidency and Quorum of the Twelve held weekly in the temple. "President Heber J. Grant," wrote Joseph Fielding Smith, "has not met with the brethren in a meeting on Thursday for many weeks. He is confined to his home most of the time, but is keen on many matters, especially everything financial."[33]

October Conference 1944

Again, my brethren, I am privileged to be with you in another general conference of the Church, and I bear testimony that I know it is by the healing and sustaining power of God that I am here. In another six or seven weeks, the Lord being willing, I shall begin the eighty-ninth year of my life; and shall have completed sixty-two years since I became one of the Apostles; and shall have served twenty-six years as President of the Church. In all this, and in much else, the Lord has blessed me richly; and I am grateful I can say that I am better now than I have been during some of the weeks and months just passed. I come to the office nearly every day, and I refrain from speaking to you now only on counsel of my doctor, whose advice I usually take.[34]

It was during the sixty-two years he served as an Apostle and prophet that Heber J. Grant witnessed a remarkable transformation in the Church that he led and loved. He had been ordained an Apostle during a time when the staunch persecution of polygamists reached it peak, and he and his three wives faced the fallout from the anti-polygamy legislation of the 1880s. With the Manifesto, which ended the practice, he had to personally accommodate himself to the new ecclesiastical order and adhere to the government's rulings while helping the Saints to do likewise. Then later during his tenure as President of Church he had to speak out against those who couldn't abide the new commands given.

As senior Apostle and prophet, President Grant guided the Church through two world wars and provided counsel during the Great Depression. He was privy to seeing the Church get out of debt and was instrumental in maintaining its financial stability.[35] It was during his watch that the Church welfare program was implemented, enabling the Church to care for its members. During his presidency he also dedicated temples in Hawaii, Arizona, and Alberta, Canada. (See appendix 2.) And though he was the first prophet who had not known Joseph Smith personally, he became linked to the Prophet as he oversaw the centennial commemorations that celebrated Moroni's initial visit, the organization of the Church, and the first missionary efforts in Great Britain.

Not only did he witness the great changes in *what* story was told about Mormonism, he was intimately involved with the change in *how* it was told. On 6 May 1922, Heber first preached the gospel via radio, reading, as part of his address, portions of Doctrine and Covenants 76. Concerning the radio Heber felt that "undoubtedly the greatest miracle of the century is the accomplishment by which the human voice, with

the personality of the speaker, may be indefinitely preserved and repro-
duced with every detail of originality. Whether uttered in the frozen
arctics, or from the jungles of the tropics, without visible means of
conduct, the human voice instantly circles the earth, thus overcoming
the hitherto insurmountable barrier of both time and space."[36]

Two years later, the October 1924 general conference was broadcast
on station KFPT (now KSL) to Saints in the western United States and
Canada, and a month later, a Sunday evening service was inaugurated
and broadcast weekly. President Grant was the speaker on numerous
occasions. It was also during his presidency that the weekly radio broadcasts of the Mormon Tabernacle Choir first began. Whereas he, as stake
president in Tooele, made laborious journeys by horseback, wagon,
buggy, and train to visit all his assigned wards and branches, by 1936,
with the first international broadcast of conference, Heber J. Grant had
witnessed astonishing changes in how the gospel could be preached.
Though the gospel was the same at his death as it had been when he
became an Apostle, the same could not be said of the Church.

President Grant broadcasts a gospel message on station KZN, 6 May 1922.

A Final Address

President Grant would give a final message to the Saints in the 1945 April conference. As had become customary, the talk had to be read by someone else, but the power of the testimony he bore was not diminished. "The most glorious thing that has ever happened in the history of the world since the Savior himself lived on earth, is that God Himself saw fit to visit the earth with His beloved, only begotten Son, our our Redeemer and Savior, and to appear to the boy Joseph. . . . I do not have the language at my command to express the gratitude to God for this knowledge that I possess. Time and time again my heart has been melted, my eyes have wept tears of gratitude for the knowledge that He lives and that this gospel called Mormonism is in very deed the plan of life and salvation, that it is in very deed the Gospel of the Lord Jesus Christ."[37]

This proved to be his final testimony, as on 14 May 1945, just days after the war in Europe ended, Heber J. Grant passed away. In the June 1945 issue, the *Improvement Era* noted his death.

> For more than one hundred months this page in the *Era* has carried messages from and news of its senior editor, Heber J. Grant, President of the Church of Jesus Christ of Latter-day Saints.
>
> Monday evening, May 14, 1945, our Father in Heaven, who measures out the days and the years of men, saw fit to relieve him of the cares of this life. But whatever the nature of the physical cares which nearly eighty-nine years of strenuous living visited upon him, in spirit there was always about him a refreshment. His was the outlook of one who knew that men may die—but never grow old. As between time and eternity it mattered little to him. Those who live there were as real to him as those who live here. And none who knew him could doubt his conviction. And now he has gone to that place which was as real to him as was this one.[38]

NOTES TO CHAPTER 9

1. *Collected Discourses,* 5:400.
2. Ronald W. Walker, "Young Heber J. Grant: Entrepreneur Extraordinary," in *The Twentieth Century American West: Contributions to an Understanding,* ed. Thomas Alexander and John F. Bluth (Provo, Utah: Charles Redd Center for Western Studies, 1983), 99–100.
3. Ibid., 100.
4. Ibid.
5. CR, October 1938, 7.
6. Ibid.
7. Ronald W. Walker, "Heber J. Grant's European Mission, 1903–1906," *Journal of Mormon History* 14 (1988): 26.
8. "A Page from the Life of a Busy Man," *IE,* February 1937, 67.
9. CR, October 1938, 7.
10. CR, April 1937, 17–18.
11. Walker, "Heber J. Grant's European Mission, 1903–1906," 19.
12. Quoted in Walker, "Heber J. Grant's European Mission, 1903–1906," 19.
13. Ibid.
14. G. Ott Romney, "A Habit Worth Acquiring," *IE,* November 1931, 16.
15. CR, October 1925, 2.
16. Heber J. Grant Diary, 19 May 1931; quoted in Richard O. Cowan, "Advice from a Prophet: Take Time Out," *BYU Studies* 16 (spring 1976), 415.
17. CR, April 1932, 8.
18. CR, October 1936, 15.
19. *The Detroit News,* 12 May 1936; quoted in Stringham A. Stevens, "The President Goes to Dearborn," *IE,* July 1936, 399.
20. D. Michael Quinn, *J. Reuben Clark: The Church Years* (Provo, Utah: Brigham Young University Press, 1983), 83.
21. Francis M. Gibbons, *Heber J. Grant: Man of Steel, Prophet of God* (Salt Lake City: Deseret Book Company, 1979), 215.
22. CR, October 1941, 6.
23. CR, April 1940, 2, 3.
24. CR, October 1940, 95.
25. Ibid., 130.
26. CR, October 1907, 24–25.

27. CR, April 1941, 128.

28. CR, October 1941, 6.

29. CR, October 1942, 24.

30. CR, April 1942, 2.

31. CR, October 1943, 9.

32. Heber J. Grant Journal, 1 July–1 December 1943; quoted in Quinn, *J. Reuben Clark: The Church Years*, 91.

33. Joseph Fielding Smith Journal, 3 June 1943; quoted in Quinn, *J. Reuben Clark: The Church Years*, 90.

34. CR, October 1944, 6.

35. Heber M. Wells, "President Grant—The Business Man," *IE*, November 1936, 689. "The part which President Grant has played in keeping the Church out of debt," according to John Wells of the Presiding Bishopric, "has been manifest in every way. He has set his face like flint against contracting obligations greater than the revenues justified, and has nurtured, protected, and greatly enhanced its assets until today the Church owes not one red cent, but on the contrary is the owner of much real estate and other valuable investments of gratifying magnitude."

36. CR, April 1930, 4.

37. CR, April 1945, 10.

38. "The Editor's Page," *IE*, June 1945, 331.

∿ APPENDIX ONE ∿

TESTIMONY of RACHEL GRANT

The following is an excerpt from the November 1930 issue of the IMPROVEMENT ERA, *which published "Statement of Rachel Ridgeway Grant"—the testimony of Heber J. Grant's mother and her personal account of the Prophet Joseph Smith.*

The first time I saw the Prophet Joseph Smith was in New Jersey, before I joined the Church. He preached there that night, but I was prejudiced at that time. I just went to hear him out of curiosity. My sister joined the Church before I did, and she wanted me to go a great many times, so finally I did go. After that I went several times to hear the "Mormons."

The Baptist minister and everyone warned me about going to hear them. He said if I did not stop going, I must give up my place in the Baptist Church; and then I went right along. I commenced to read the *Voice of Warning* and the Book of Mormon. I read nearly all night in the Book of Mormon, and felt that it was true, and then I got the spirit of gathering and went to Nauvoo.

I was many times at the Prophet's house, but not so many times when I saw him. We used to have parties there.

He was not at home very much. His life was so often sought that he had to be hid up. After he had been in hiding and had come out, he was always jolly and happy. He would play with the people, and he was always cheerful and happy whenever he would come out. He was different in that respect from Brother Hyrum, who was more sedate, more serious. I thought at the time Hyrum seemed more like a prophet than Joseph did. You see there was a great deal of sectarianism about me. I thought it was bad to sing or read a newspaper on Sunday. Once when a schoolmate of mine had come down from Trenton and wanted me to go with her to hear the "Mormons," I went Saturday, but did not want to go on Sunday at all. But I thought it would be impolite not to do as she wished, so I went. When I came home I went right upstairs and asked the Lord to forgive me for going to hear them on Sunday.

I guess you have seen the picture where Brother Joseph was preaching to the Indians. I was there at that time. The Indians were all kneeling down on the grass in front of the Mansion, and if you have seen that picture, that just describes the way everything was, though it is a miserable picture of the Prophet. He was a fine, noble looking man, always so neat. There are some of the pictures that do not look a particle like him. When he was preaching you could feel the power and influence.

The first year I was in Nauvoo was a happy year, but after that it was all confusion. When the press was burned there was such excitement; it was that way all the time. It tried a great many people when the Prophet gave out the word that there was to be no more gathering at Nauvoo, as the people thought that was the place. He first told them to gather there, but later told them the Rocky Mountains would be the gathering place. It was his thought that they would come to the Rocky Mountains.

I was in Nauvoo when the Prophet went to Carthage, and when his body was brought back. I had come to Nauvoo in 1842, and came home to New Jersey in the fall of 1844.

After the Prophet's death when Sidney Ridgon came to Nauvoo and spoke, he thought that it was his right and privilege to be President of the Church. President Young jumped right up on the seat and spoke. If you had had your eyes shut, you would have thought it was the Prophet. In fact he looked like him, his very countenance seemed to change, and he spoke like him.

I know Joseph Smith was a Prophet, and I have lived to see many of his sayings fulfilled.

～ APPENDIX TWO ～

"Temple Work Should Be Done," an article excerpted here from the IMPROVEMENT ERA, *November 1941, was written by Rachel Grant Taylor, Heber J. Grant's daughter. It relates President Grant's involvement in latter-day temple work. The title of the article was taken from the flyleaf of one of Heber J. Grant's journals.*

There is a special chapter in Father's life which is woven and interwoven into the pattern of all his eighty-five years. That chapter concerns his vital interest in the temples of the Church and the work carried on within their walls.

Father was not born in the shadow of a temple, for in 1856, the temple walls were themselves deep in the shadow of their foundation trenches. The Temple Square was one of his childhood playgrounds. Of those days he says: "I can remember the temple when I was just a little child. I used to play on the walls when they were only three or four feet high." How little did he or anyone dream that some day he would preside within its sacred precincts!

It was interesting to him to watch a yoke of oxen hauling a mammoth stone swung by a chain from the axle between the two wheels, then to see the stone-cutters shape and smooth the granite block to fill a predetermined spot in the temple wall.

His eyes have seen every structure on Salt Lake City's Main Street grow from nothing to its present stature. Many buildings have come and gone, but not so the temple: firm-rooted, massive, time-defying, it stood, after forty years of slow, painstaking growth had culminated in the beauty of its sky-flung spires. To him, as to all others who lived in the "City of the Saints," it was and will always be the center of their compass—streets north, east, south, and west all measured from the square on which it stands.

Father has attended the dedication of the Logan, Manti, and Salt Lake temples, and as President of the Church he has offered the dedicatory prayer at the Alberta, Hawaiian, and Mesa temples. He has selected the site for the Los Angeles Temple, and personally set aside $5,000 towards its erection. He looks forward with keen anticipation to the time when the Idaho Falls Temple will be dedicated and has given $5,000 toward that building. He has always wanted to feel that he "owned" a part of each of the temples of the Church.

From his young manhood, he has been active in raising funds for these sacred buildings. A year before the dedication of the St. George Temple, every ward in Salt Lake Valley held parties to raise funds for that building. Bishop Woolley gave Father the special call to make the Thirteenth Ward the leading one in this effort.

Of his personal contributions he says:

> When I was making $25 a month, I paid 25 cents to the temple. As my earning increased, I increased the amount of my donation, until I was giving $5 a month to the temple. The 30th Quorum of Seventies, of which I was made a member when nineteen years of age, had a stone-cutter working on the Temple Block. We paid him a regular salary each month, and my share was $5. [The old record book of this quorum credits Father with $76 from December, 1876, to September, 1877].

At the time of the final drive for contributions to complete the Salt Lake Temple, father was sent to Tooele stake with a list of names followed by the amount requested. Every man except one answered the call. Father's donation credited to Tooele stake was $1,500.

Father was an ambitious boy, and he decided on three important objectives which he desired to reach by the time he was twenty-one years of age—(1) to establish a business of his own, (2) to build a home for his mother, and (3) to get married. He was successful in all three. If he had not been so busy with his first and third objectives, he might have accompanied his mother when she went to St. George the year the temple there was dedicated. Instead, he devoted himself to courting my mother, Lucy Stringham.

In a letter telling of their marriage he writes:

> I went to St. George to be married because the temple there had been completed, and the old Endowment House had been closed. Marriages were being performed by the presidents of stakes and bishops, with the understanding that the young people would later, of course, go to the St. George Temple and be sealed. I said: "I don't want any of this being sealed later on. I want to be married properly to start out with."

> Some of my friends tried to persuade me to be married by the bishop and then wait for the completion of the Salt Lake Temple to be sealed to your mother. I have always rejoiced that I did not follow their advice, because she died before the temple was dedicated.

> The trip from Salt Lake to St. George was a fair drive to make in ten days. Going as we did by train to Santaquin, we saved a little over two days. It took us nearly a week to get from Salt Lake to St. George. From Santaquin we went the rest of the trip in Uncle Erastus Snow's white top.

> We were entertained on our way to St. George by the people who entertained Erastus Snow. Some of the roads near St. George, over the Black Hills, were very rough. Indeed, it seemed as though we would jump from one rock to another.

> There were no restaurants in those days and we had our meals at the homes of the Saints. I met a great many people who expressed pleasure at entertaining me as a son of Jedediah M. Grant. I do not recall in the same length of time that I ever heard so many kind expressions regarding my father as I did on that trip.

In St. George we stayed at the big Snow house, and were married by Uncle Erastus; your mother did not want anyone else to perform the ceremony. She said that next to her father, Briant Stringham, Apostle Erastus Snow was her ideal.

I was married November 1, 1877—twenty-one days before I was twenty-one.

I have never regretted taking the long trip to St. George to be married, and I shed tears of gratitude years later when the members of the Young Women's M. I. A. Board were strongly urging our young people to go to the temple to be married, and I heard you express your gratitude that you had been born under the seal of the covenant. We always get our reward sooner or later when we do our duty in the Church. I am sure that my going to St. George to be married in the temple has had a strong effect for good upon my children.

Today Father could add a postscript to this letter to me, expressing the joy he must feel that his ten children and seventeen of his grandchildren have followed his example and been married in a sacred temple.

The first temple dedication in which Father was privileged to participate was in Logan. He tells how on Wednesday, May 14, 1884, he, Mother, and their baby daughter, Florence, joined the party of thirty-five who were accompanying President John Taylor. The following Saturday morning the services were held, with President John Taylor offering the dedicatory prayer. Father writes:

The services were held in the large hall in the upper part of the building, and after they were over the congregation passed through other portions of the building, led by President Taylor, his Counselors, and the Apostles. . . .

> I shall make no attempt at a description of the Logan Temple, other than to say that it has been finished in much better style than I had expected and is a building that the Saints can justly point to with commendable feelings of pride and satisfaction, and especially is this the case with reference to those portions of the people that have contributed for the erection of the building, either by labor or with their means. It gives me a feeling of satisfaction to know that I have done something, viz., $300, in this direction. . . .

> Today has been a time of rejoicing with the Latter-day Saints and one long to be remembered by those having the privilege of attending the dedication services.

Father's journal for Wednesday, May 21, 1884, tells of going to the temple at 8 A.M. with Mother to witness the first day's work. He was called upon to assist in the setting apart of Marriner W. Merrill, who had been chosen as president of the temple. After seeing a number of baptisms in the font room, Father was asked to act as witness for the first two marriages.

Father's account of the dedication of the Manti Temple four years later covers thirty-four pages in his journal. It shows a picture very different from the carefree days at Logan. Underlying the deep joy of presenting to God another temple was the tragedy of persecution which kept President Wilford Woodruff and many other leaders in hiding, preventing them from participating fully with the Saints. It was a time that called for real faith on the part of a humble and chastened people. Father's words reveal that for him those days spent in the Manti Temple were replete with satisfying spiritual experiences.

Tuesday, May 16, 1888, Father records that the dedicatory prayer was read by George Reynolds at a private meeting and was accepted on motion of F. M. Lyman.

On Thursday, May 17, he records:

> Met in the temple at 10. A.M., with twenty-nine of the brethren, including myself.

This meeting for the private dedication was called to order by President Woodruff at 12 o'clock. After singing "The Morning Breaks," President Woodruff offered the Dedicatory Prayer. Of the President's remarks Father writes:

> He referred to his attending a testimony meeting in the days of the Prophet Joseph when the Prophet said they (the brethren present) were but children in the knowledge of the greatness of the work of God, and what it was to accomplish. Said this work (Mormonism) would fill North and South America, and there would yet be tens of thousands of Saints in the Rocky Mountains. "Here I am, fifty-four years after hearing the Prophet make this statement, located in the Rocky Mountains." . . . "From the beginning both earth and hell have united against this Kingdom. I have no doubts of this work arriving at its perfection. There is no power that can stay it. Our government is taking our property, and I cannot say what the result will be, but I have earnestly prayed to the Lord that our temples might be preserved and I have a strong testimony that our enemies will not take our temples. . . ."

On Friday morning at a meeting of the authorities, Father was one who assisted in setting apart Daniel H. Wells as president of the temple. Of Monday, May 21, he writes:

> The Dedication Services started at 10:55, just one hour after the opening of the doors. . . . Brother Lorenzo Snow spoke and asked us to prepare our hearts by bowing both our heads and our hearts before the Lord so that we might get the spirit while the dedicatory prayer was offered.

Father names the sixteen men who spoke during the services, and reports some of their remarks. He was especially interested in the testimonies of Patriarch John Smith and William Cahoon who told of being present at the dedication of the Kirtland and Nauvoo Temples.

Father records his feelings and gratitude at the close of this day with these words:

> I am glad to feel that I have a substantial interest in the Manti Temple. I have donated over $900 to aid in its erection. This amount is not all credited to me, as part of it stands in the names of my wives and children, and some in my mother's. It is my intention to make the actual amount paid by me up to $1,000, as I would like about that much of an interest in the building.
>
> I have been abundantly blessed of the Lord financially, and I wish to show my gratitude to Him by doing my full share in aiding public enterprises. I have done pretty well in the past, and hope for power and the disposition to continue to do something in the future.

At the close of Tuesday's meeting, Father wrote these words of gratitude and self-examination:

> Today we have had a greater flow of the Spirit than yesterday. I had no idea yesterday that it would be possible to have a better time and yet today has been much better than yesterday. Many of the Saints have had manifestations today. Today has been the most enjoyable of my life. . . . Many times during the services of the past three days tears of gratitude to God for His goodness and mercy to me have filled my eyes. The dedication of the Manti Temple has been the greatest spiritual treat of my life, and I hope and pray for strength from on high to enable me to continue faithful to the work of God.
>
> When I think of those that have fallen who have had many greater testimonies than I have, I realize my weakness, and my inability to stand unless I shall have the aid of my Heavenly Father. . . .

We have indeed had a time of rejoicing, and I would that all Israel could have been present to partake of the heavenly influence that has been with us.

All his life Father had looked forward to the time of the dedication of the Salt Lake Temple, yet as the date drew near, it was only by a few hours' margin that he reached the city. He writes:

Upon my return from Washington, where I had been detained on account of the sickness of my daughters Rachel and Lucy (Lucy was sick nigh unto death and it was miraculous that she was healed) my wife and my brother met me in Chicago. In case the girls were not able to travel they were going to stay there and I was going to come on to Salt Lake City to be here for the dedication of the temple. However, the girls stood the trip to Chicago well, and we arrived, as I remember it, at 3 o'clock in the morning of April 6, 1893.

Members of the Church who question being interviewed in order to receive a temple recommend may be surprised to find that the same procedure at that time applied to the Twelve Apostles. At the time of the dedication of the Salt Lake Temple, Father says:

Prior to the morning meeting in the temple I was interviewed by Brother Francis M. Lyman at the request of Lorenzo Snow, President of the Council of the Twelve. It seems that all of the brethren, each and every one, had been interviewed and had to pledge himself to keep all the commandments of the Lord—the law of tithing, the Word of Wisdom, etc.—before they would be admitted into the temple for the dedication. Brother Lyman called at my home and told me of this, and that President Lorenzo Snow had vouched for me as being worthy, and that it was unnecessary to have me interviewed, which pleased me very much.

In a letter Father writes:

> We have been forty years building the temple, and I would
> not have missed being here for anything, as I have been
> donating something each year for more than twenty years
> to assist in its erection.

> Dedication services have been held in the temple fourteen
> times, and perhaps 25,000 people have attended. The hall
> holds something over 2,000, and there has been a different
> audience at each meeting.

For the dedication of the Hawaiian temple, Father and his accompanying party arrived in Honolulu on November 21, 1919. The
following day the Saints celebrated his sixty-third birthday with a big
feast at Laie. A bounteous spread such as the Hawaiians are masters in
preparing was served to all. As a birthday remembrance, President
Nibley gave Father the diamond tie pin which he has worn ever since.

The dedicatory services were held on Thanksgiving Day. Despite
the joy of the occasion, in Father's heart there was an ever-recurring
note of sadness. His first words were:

> I cannot express to you the keen sorrow which I feel that I
> have to offer this dedicatory prayer instead of President
> Joseph F. Smith. It was, I am sure, one of the fondest
> dreams of his life that he might be here at the dedication of
> this temple, . . . but in the providence of the Lord he has
> been taken from us, and this duty, or I might say this high
> honor and great pleasure, has come to me.

Later he said:

> I am very grateful indeed to my Heavenly Father for the
> rich outpouring of His Spirit at each and all of the meet-
> ings we have held in this holy place. I feel the assurance in
> my heart that this temple has been accepted of the Lord
> and that His spirit will dwell here. . . . We believe it is

absolutely acceptable to the Lord, and that it is acceptable to Presidents Cannon and Smith, and to the faithful men and women who have labored on these islands and have gone on before.

After the final dedication services, Father set apart President William M. Waddoups as president of the temple.

For the dedication of the Alberta Temple a special train with a party of one hundred sixty left Salt Lake, August 23, 1923, for Cardston, Alberta, Canada. Two days later they arrived.

On Sunday, Monday, and Tuesday it would appear that there were three services held each day, and on Wednesday there were two, after which the temple was opened for ordinance work for those who had come some distance. On this occasion he said:

> I remember as well as I remember anything that ever happened in my life the thrill that went through my very being, the joy and satisfaction I experienced when President Smith stood up in the Tabernacle and announced that a temple was to be erected in Canada. There are times in our lives when something comes into our souls in the nature, we might say, almost of an electric shock, that thrills our being, and when we are thrilled by the Spirit of the living God, as I feel that audience was at the time of the announcement of the prospective erection of this building, we have not the language with which to express to God our gratitude for His blessings to us on such occasions. . . .

> I have been particularly grateful that although I read the prayer eleven times, I did not weary of it, and it did not become tiresome, and I seemed to have the spirit of prayer each time that I read it.

> The still small voice of revelation to our spirits is the thing that counts, not seeing great manifestations, not seeing angels, not speaking in tongues, not great visions. Since I

became an Apostle some of the men who have been more wonderfully and abundantly blessed with great manifestations than any of the others with whom I have been associated have lost their faith. Why? Because they did not learn one lesson, which is the greatest of all the lessons that any Latter-day Saint can learn, and that lesson is that "obedience is better than sacrifice, and to hearken than the fat of rams."

On October 20, 1927, we took the train for Los Angeles en route to the dedication of the Arizona Temple. There were two special cars containing nearly all of the General Authorities and their wives, and others who were going to the dedication at Mesa.

Father said on October 22:

Attended the dedication service at 10 A.M., and 2 and 7 P.M. The dedicatory prayer is practically identical with the prayers I offered at the Hawaiian and Cardston temples. I felt impressed in Hawaii that I had been inspired when I sat down with Brother Arthur Winter and dictated the prayer for the Hawaiian Temple, and therefore neither at Canada nor at Arizona have I made any special effort to change that prayer. . . .

You can be Saviors upon Mt. Zion by laboring in the temples. To my mind one of the greatest and grandest and most glorious of all the labors that anyone can be engaged in is laboring for the salvation of the souls of their loved ones, their ancestors who have gone before, who had not the privilege of listening to the Gospel and embracing it.

Upon one occasion I heard President Wilford Woodruff announce that there would be very few souls for whom the people performed ordinances in the temples of God, who,

> when they heard the Gospel preached to them beyond the
> veil, would not accept of the vicarious work.
>
> I thank the Lord for having had the great pleasure of being
> present at the dedication of the Logan, Manti, Salt Lake,
> and Hawaiian temples, and now of being present here. I
> wish to bear witness to you in all of those services God has
> seen fit to bless His servants and to inspire them in
> speaking to the people, and that there has been a spirit of
> peace, joy and happiness and testimony present in each
> and all of these six houses dedicated to God.

To take part in the dedication of six of the temples erected in
Western America was a privilege which came to Father because of his
high callings as an Apostle and President of the Church. But the privilege of using a temple for eternal marriage and for carrying on sacred
ordinance work for a family is one given to all faithful members of
the Church.

The record of the last forty years has demonstrated how thoroughly Father has taken advantage of that privilege. In 1901 he gave a
Grant record to Joseph Christenson at the Salt Lake Temple, asking
him to prepare the names for temple work. From that day until today
he has had someone working along research lines. For almost ten
years Grace Roberts Reynolds, a trained research worker, has been in
charge of the family records. Mrs. Reynolds' powers have been taxed
to capacity, especially at times when Father employed as many as
twenty-five or thirty persons, some of whom attended three and four
temple sessions a day.

The St. George Temple record of 1883 shows work performed by
Father. Aunt Augusta made going to the temple a regular part of her
weekly program. Father says it was her faithful labors that finally
made him realize that he too should participate in the work. My sister
Lucy and I went to the temple much younger than girls of today are
allowed to go. We spent many long, peaceful days together taking
part in the spiritual ceremonies conducted in the beautiful rooms of
our beloved temple.

For a number of years Father sang in the temple choir at the request of Professor Charles J. Thomas who had once thought that singing for Father was not in the realm of possibility.

It was in January, 1928, while I was in the Northern States mission with my husband that Father's active personal participation in temple work began. He sent letters of invitation to all the members of the family and set apart Thursday night as temple night for the Grant "clan." I remember upon our return when we joined the group, how inspiring it was to see fifteen, twenty, and sometimes more than thirty of the family who had responded to his call.

Uncle Morgan and Uncle Hyrum Grant's families were most faithful in coming. A busy man like the late Dr. Frederick J. Pack was very seldom absent. I like to remember how many nights President Rudger Clawson was at the sessions we attended.

Figures commonly represent dollars and cents, but figures to the temple worker are the pigment that portrays most vividly the picture of work accomplished. The totals of Father's, Mother's, and Aunt Augusta's work as recorded in Father's record up to September 18, 1941, show that there are 232 pages of pedigree charts, 12,415 family group sheets, and that 51,995 baptisms and 51,995 endowments have been completed, 9,635 husbands and wives have been sealed, and 31,744 children have been sealed to parents.

The total of temple ordinances reaches to 145,369.

At the temple Joseph Christenson has viewed with keen delight the progress of the work, and A. F. Bennett, secretary of the Genealogical Society, says in a letter dated September 16, 1941:

> In all the Church there is no other individual who has succeeded in tracing so many of his ancestral lines back to ancient times as has President Grant. It has been most remarkable how records have come to light as the search for his progenitors continued unremittingly.
>
> An effort has also been made to follow down descendants on all these various lines. Therefore practically all temple work done by President Grant for his family has been for known relatives who are connected up in lineal pedigrees. It is probable that no other family in the Church has

accomplished so much in connected genealogical research
and in the total of temple ordinances administered.

Father's love of his fellowmen, expressed in helping the living as well as saving the dead, has been a vital element in bringing about this impressive temple record. As I think of the number of souls touched through this work, I visualize a city of over sixty thousand happy people of all ages on the other side.

Father has been building the bridge from time to eternity, and when in years to come he crosses over that bridge, what a multitude will be waiting to bid him welcome!

⌒ ABOUT THE AUTHOR ⌒

Matthew J. Haslam was born in Provo, Utah, but spent his growing-up years in Los Angeles, then in San Diego. He graduated from the University of North Carolina in Greensboro, with a Ph.D. in Rhetoric and Composition, and has taught at Brigham Young University. Matt enjoys backpacking and fly-fishing, and presently resides in Orem, Utah, with his wife, Jeanne, and their three children.

~ PHOTO CREDITS ~

p. 14   Jedediah Morgan Grant. Photographer: Savage & Ottinger.

p. 17   Heber J. and Rachel Ridgeway Ivins Grant.

p. 24   Heber J. Grant and his brothers, courtesy of the Church Archives, The Church of Jesus Christ of Latter-day Saints.

p. 31   Heber Jeddy Grant, photograph of daguerreotype.

p. 33   Heber J. Grant as a young man, courtesy of the Church Archives, The Church of Jesus Christ of Latter-day Saints.

p. 70   The family of Heber J. and Lucy Stringham Grant, courtesy of the Church Archives, The Church of Jesus Christ of Latter-day Saints.

p. 80   Augusta Winters Grant, courtesy of the Church Archives, The Church of Jesus Christ of Latter-day Saints.

p. 85   Heber J. Grant and his wife Emily Wells Grant, courtesy of the Church Archives, The Church of Jesus Christ of Latter-day Saints.

p. 95   Heber J. Grant, courtesy of the Church Archives, The Church of Jesus Christ of Latter-day Saints.

p. 114   Heber J. Grant's ten daughters, courtesy of the Church Archives, The Church of Jesus Christ of Latter-day Saints.

EXCERPTS FROM
TEACHINGS OF THE PROPHET
JOSEPH SMITH

A quarter of a century ago, Elder Edwin F. Parry compiled and published a classified arrangement of excerpts from doctrinal sermons and writings of the Prophet Joseph Smith. These sayings were taken from the Documentary History of the Church. That little work filled an important mission, but left in the hearts and minds of all who were interested in the sayings of the great latter-day Prophet, a longing for more of his sayings, which longing was not satisfied. Many faithful members of the Church have expressed the desire that a more extensive work of this kind be published. The members of the Church quite generally desire to know what the Prophet Joseph Smith may have said on important subjects, for they look upon his utterances as coming through divine inspiration.

Many of these discourses and writings appear in the Documentary History of the Church, but others have not been included in these volumes, but are scattered through the early publications of the Church. It has been difficult even for the student to obtain these because the old publications are not accessible for general use.

In accordance with the many calls that have been made that there be a more extensive compilation of these discourses and sayings, the matter was taken up in the Historian's Office and such a compilation has been prepared, submitted to the First Presidency, and passed by them for publication.

It should be remembered that this compilation contains some discourses and statements from the minutes of council and priesthood meetings, which are not verbatim reports of the Prophet's remarks, but which have been approved in those minutes. There has been no attempt to compile these sayings by subject, because frequently in the same article or discourse, several subjects are discussed. It has been thought best to give each article, or portion of article, chronologically, with an exhaustive index through which the various subjects may be found. Historical matters and incidental or unimportant matters have been eliminated. By the use of asterisks these portions left out are indicated in the body of the work.

Articles which are accessible, such as *Joseph Smith Tells His Own Story*, which as been published in tract form and also in the Pearl of Great Price, are not added to this work. References have been made to the revelations in the Doctrine and Covenants where necessary, but these revelations are not included in this work.

It is felt that this volume will meet a need and promote faith among the members of the Church. With this intent it is sent out on its mission as another testimony of the divine calling of the Prophet Joseph Smith.

JOSEPH FIELDING SMITH
Church Historian.

SEARCH THE REVELATIONS OF GOD

The following excerpts are taken from the second number of the *Evening and Morning Star,* published in August, 1832. The article from which these thoughts are taken was prepared by the Prophet and published in this issue of the *Star.*

Search the scriptures—search the revelations which we publish, and ask your Heavenly Father, in the name of His Son Jesus Christ, to manifest the truth unto you, and if you do it with an eye single to his glory nothing doubting, He will answer you by the power of His Holy Spirit. You will then know for yourselves and not for another. You will not then be dependent on man for the knowledge of God; nor will there be any room for speculation. No; for when men receive their instruction from Him that made them, they know how He will save them. Then again we say: Search the scriptures, search the Prophets and learn what portion of them belongs to you and the people of the nineteenth century. You, no doubt, will agree with us, and say, that you have no right to claim the promises of the inhabitants before the flood; that you cannot found your hopes of salvation upon the obedience of the children of Israel when journeying in the wilderness, nor can you expect that the blessings which the apostles pronounced upon the churches of Christ eighteen hundred years ago, were intended for you. Again, if others' blessings are not your blessings, others' curses are not your curses; you stand then in these last days, as all have stood before you, agents unto yourselves, to be judged according to your works.

EVERY MAN AN AGENT FOR HIMSELF

Every man lives for himself. Adam was made to open the way of the world, and for dressing the garden. Noah was born to save seed of everything, when the earth was washed of its wickedness by the flood; and the Son of God came into the world to redeem it from the fall. But except a man be born again, he cannot see the kingdom of God. This eternal truth settles the question of all men's religion. A man may be saved, after the judgment, in the terrestrial kingdom, or in the telestial kingdom, but he can never see the celestial kingdom of God, without being born of water and the Spirit. He may receive a glory like unto the moon, [i.e., of which the light of the moon is typical], or a star, [i.e., of which the light of the stars is typical], but he can never come unto Mount Zion, and unto the city of the living God, the heavenly Jerusalem, and to an innumerable company of angels; to the general assembly and Church of the Firstborn, which are written in heaven, and to God the judge of all, and to the spirits of just men made perfect, and to Jesus the Mediator of the new covenant, unless he becomes as a little child, and is taught by the Spirit of God. Wherefore, we again say, search the revelations of God; study the prophecies, and rejoice that God grants unto the world Seers and Prophets. They are they who saw the mysteries of godliness; they saw the flood before it came; they saw angels ascending and descending upon a ladder that reached from earth to heaven; they saw the stone cut out of the mountain, which filled the whole earth; they saw the

Son of God come from the regions of bliss and dwell with men on earth; they saw the deliverer come out of Zion, and turn away ungodliness from Jacob; they saw the glory of the Lord when he showed the transfiguration of the earth on the mount; they saw every mountain laid low and every valley exalted when the Lord was taking vengeance upon the wicked; they saw truth spring out of the earth, and righteousness look down from heaven in the last days, before the Lord came the second time to gather his elect; they saw the end of wickedness on earth, and the Sabbath of creation crowned with peace; they saw the end of the glorious thousand years, when Satan was loosed for a little season; they saw the day of judgment when all men received according to their works, and they saw the heaven and the earth flee away to make room for the city of God, when the righteous receive an inheritance in eternity. And, fellow sojourners upon earth, it is your privilege to purify yourselves and come up to the same glory, and see for yourselves, and know for yourselves. Ask, and it shall be given you; seek and ye shall find; knock, and it shall be opened unto you. —*E&MS* August, 1832. *DHC* 1:282–284.

LETTER TO EDITOR SAXTON

January 4, 1833, the Prophet wrote to Mr. N. E. Saxton, an editor of a newspaper, the following words of counsel and warning concerning the state of the world and the purpose of the Lord in the restoration spoken of by the ancient prophets.

❧

Kirtland, January 4th, 1833.

Mr. Editor:—Sir, Considering the liberal principles upon which your interesting and valuable paper is published, myself being a subscriber, and feeling a deep interest in the cause of Zion, and in the happiness of my brethren of mankind, I cheerfully take up my pen to contribute my mite at this very interesting and important period.

For some length of time I have been carefully viewing the state of things, as it now appears, throughout our Christian land; and have looked at it with feelings of the most painful anxiety. While upon one hand I behold the manifest withdrawal of God's Holy Spirit, and the veil of stupidity which seems to be drawn over the hearts of the people; upon the other hand, I behold the judgments of God that have swept, and are still sweeping hundreds and thousands of our race, and I fear unprepared, down to the shades of death. With this solemn and alarming fact before me, I am led to exclaim, "O that my head were waters, and mine eyes a fountain of tears, that I might weep day and night."

A Sleeping Christianity

I think that it is high time for a Christian world to awake out of sleep, and cry mightily to that God, day and night, whose anger we have justly incurred. Are not these things a sufficient stimulant to arouse the faculties, and call forth the energies of every man, woman, or child that possesses feelings of sympathy for their fellows, or that is in any degree endeared to the budding cause of our glorious Lord? I leave an intelligent community to answer this important question, with a confession, that this is what has caused me to overlook my own inability, and expose my weakness to a learned world; but, trusting in that God who has said that these things are hid from the wise and prudent and revealed unto babes, I step forth into the field to tell you what the Lord is doing, and what you must do, to enjoy the smiles of your Savior in these last days.

The Covenant with Israel

The time has at last arrived when the God of Abraham, of Isaac, and of Jacob, has set his hand again the second time to recover the remnants of his people, which have been left from Assyria, and from Egypt, and from Pathros, and from Cush, and from Elam, and from Shinar, and from Hamath, and from the islands of the sea, and with them to bring in the fulness of the Gentiles, and establish that covenant with them, which was promised when their sins should be taken away. See Isaiah 6; Romans 6:25, 26 and 27; and also Jeremiah 31:31, 32 and 33. This covenant has never been established with the house of Israel, nor with the house of Judah, for it requires two parties to make a covenant, and those two parties must be agreed, or no covenant can be made.

Christ, in the days of His flesh, proposed to make a covenant with them, but they rejected Him and His proposals, and in consequence thereof, they were broken off, and no covenant was made with them at that time. But their unbelief has not rendered the promise of God of none effect: no, for there was another day limited in David, which was the day of His power; and then His people, Israel, should be a willing people;—and He would write His law in their hearts, and print it in their thoughts; their sins and their iniquities He would remember no more.

THE COVENANT TO THE GENTILES

Thus after this chosen family had rejected Christ and His proposals, the heralds of salvation said to them, "Lo we turn unto the Gentiles;" and the Gentiles received the covenant, and were grafted in from whence the chosen family were broken off; but the Gentiles have not continued in the goodness of God, but have departed from the faith that was once delivered to the Saints, and have broken the covenant in which their fathers were established (see Isa. 24:5); and have become high-minded, and have not feared; therefore, but few of them will be gathered with the chosen family. Have not the pride, high-mindedness, and unbelief of the Gentiles, provoked the Holy One of Israel to withdraw His Holy Spirit from them, and send forth His judgments to scourge them for their wickedness? This is certainly the case.